Education Uncensored

EDUCATION UnCENSORED

A Guide for the Aspiring, the Foolhardy,
and the Disillusioned

by Laurie Block Spigel

HomeschoolNYC
New York

Cover design: Kalman A. Spigel
Cover photo: Laurie Block Spigel
Game Day in Laurie's Make Your Own Board
Game class, fall 2000
Back cover photo: Gerald I. Spigel
Copyright © 2009 Laurie Block Spigel
All rights reserved.
ISBN 978-0-615-32529-3
First Edition, October 2009
Published by HomeschoolNYC
Printed in Canada

This book is dedicated to:

the Aspiring,
for all who seek to educate ourselves and our children
aspire to a higher level,

the Foolhardy,
for all who begin an adventure are fools at the start,
and there is no adventure greater than education and
parenting,

and to the Disillusioned,
who have been hurt and saddened by education
in our society today.

Table of Contents

ACKNOWLEDGEMENTS

I wish to thank many individuals who helped me with *Education Uncensored*. Daniel Judah Sklar gave me his indispensable guidance and editorial good sense. Joanna Lodin was a constant source of support. Ellen Labiner deserves thanks for carefully going over every chapter and penning me her helpful thoughts. Kaye McFarland generously contributed her story and her honest and supportive response to this book. Marcello Rubin gave me the feedback that inspired me to write the final chapter. Michael Frederic offered many helpful comments. Jennifer Dees gave me her editorial expertise and many ideas for the final revision. Heather Wood was a superlative copyeditor and formatter. Kalman gave his talents to the cover design. Heartfelt thanks go to Jim Hooson for inspiring me to finish this book. I send a big thank you to Elba Marrero and all the parents and teachers who gave me great stories and ideas, and to my many wonderful students, fellow NYCHEA members and homeschooling families who continue to give me so much. Most of all, thanks to Jerry, Kalman, and Solomon, for their unending support, and for their marvelous stories.

A Syllabus for Syllabi

Across the table from me is my mother. She balances countless classes for the home schooled children here in New York City, private classes for their parents, art courses, improv classes, and countless other things. She's currently writing the book you have in your hands. I sit across from her and can't help but smile. Here is a woman who put my book ahead of her own, and I think to myself, "She taught me well."

My mother teaches people how to teach. She does it well. She taught me how to teach. So I'm teaching her how to publish.

The first lesson she taught me is a simple one. It's the kind of lesson you find in old kung fu movies. It's the sort of lesson you wouldn't expect to hear with earnest: the greatest teachers learn from their students.

This simple and monumental lesson created an unusual and almost symbiotic relationship between us. As I learned, she learned. As she discovered, I discovered. We grew together. We shared our struggles and our victories and many of our failures.

The second thing I learned from my mother was the power of language. I was born from words. My mother wrote stories for me and filled my brain with poetry and turns of phrase. Even today I take great pleasure in using words in ways unforeseen. My mother taught me not the importance of words, but the enjoyment. And she taught me this by enjoying them herself. In this way I learned from my teacher and my teacher learned from me.

My book is published this month, a month before my mother's. We are born as writers at the same time. I'm being interviewed and I am being forced to look back over my life a lot. I get asked a lot of the same questions. People like to segregate me because I was homeschooled.

My response is very simple. It's a point my mother makes both subtly and directly inside this book. "Can you," I ask, "tell me one thing you learned in grade-school that you find important today?" and I don't mean things that a teacher told you after class, or how to deal with social situations, because those things most people learned in spite of school.

I have a friend who is a brilliant scientist on the forefront of nanotechnology. He learned all the important stuff on his own after school. I have another friend who is an award winning jazz composer. He certainly didn't learn that behind a desk. The people who are grand, gifted and special are so because they have support, because somebody takes the time to teach them on their own terms. When the only person left doing that is the person themselves they have so much less of a chance.

People have told me my entire life that this is just the way the world is, that we have to learn to function inside it. The last lesson that my mom taught me, that last big one, is that this is a copout. There is no excuse for giving into a world of mediocrity, save mediocrity itself.

I'm sure I learned more from my mother than she intended to teach. Many of my lessons were not lessons she had planned. Even more were likely lessons she had intended to avoid. But I know that I've managed to come out ahead of the curve. It's not because the curve wasn't built for me, but because the curve wasn't built for anyone.

— Kalman Spigel

Part One

I Become an Educator

The Professor's Daughter

When I was eight years old my mother took me and my sister to work. She marched us into one of her classes, on a day we had off from school, and told me to do something I had never done before. I was to act out my own teacher's misdeeds. Here, in front of a roomful of student teachers at Hunter College, I was asked to do the unthinkable: to openly malign a source of daily authority. What other child had such a rare opportunity offered to her? Obediently, I stood in front of the college classroom and pretended to be my fourth grade teacher as she handed out report cards. I stood stiff and tall, though I might have been four feet, and slowly, perhaps even threatening, walked up and down the aisles between the students. Suddenly I wheeled around to face one young man, saying, "Billy, why can't you be more like Sheryl over here (gesturing to a nearby female student), who got all Excellents?" To the class in general, I added, in a low, scolding voice, "Billy got all Unsatisfactories!" I continued to walk the aisles. "And what about Sally here?" I pointed to another student. "Sally, you got an Unsatisfactory in math, but Arthur over here got an Excellent! Why can't you be more like him?"

Afterwards some of my mother's students came

up to talk to me. Most of them simply didn't believe me. "Does your teacher really do that?" they asked. Yes, indeed she did. In fact, she did this every report card period, and there were four each year. My mother finished the lesson, pointing out that teachers should never compare students to one another and humiliation is not a motivational tool.

Yet at home my mother didn't practice what she preached. As a teacher she was absolutely right. So right, in fact, that she thought she was infallible. But as a parent, she was lacking. I might not have been compared to the student in the aisle next to me, but I had worse to live up to. My parents constantly adhered to ridiculously high standards. I was supposed to be perfect in all things, the absolute best. It took me fifty years to realize that perfection was an unattainable goal. This insidious comparison to the best, the most intelligent or talented, the most famous or successful, left me feeling a constant failure. Whenever I approached anything I enjoyed, I found myself silently comparing myself to the incomparable. I loved to paint, but could I ever be another Picasso? I loved to write, but could I ever be another Hemingway?

Even when I had reached adulthood, my mother continued to point out my failures to me. At age thirty, I received a letter from her that expressed the depth of her disappointment in me. Flush with the happiness and success of the birth of a fine baby boy, I was emotionally shattered to read how devastated my mother was over my choice to stay home and raise the child. In her letter she accused me of throwing my life away. Why, I "could have been Chief Editor of the *New York Times*,

Chancellor of NYC Schools..." and a list of other jobs that seemed to me not just unattainable, but also undesirable. (Who, I thought, in their right mind, would want to be Chancellor of NYC Schools?) My mother could never stop comparing me to what she thought I was supposed to become. No matter how hard I worked, how steadfastly I held to my own ideals, in my mother's eyes, I remained a failure.

My sister and I obediently demonstrated for my mother's education class in Hunter College whenever we had a holiday and she didn't. At age eight I taught my mother's college students how to write a research report, while my younger sister taught them about the Pilgrims. Another day my mother told her class that she had taken her children to see the Broadway musical *South Pacific*. The students, citing our young age, declared that it was an utter waste. We couldn't possibly have understood the play, they said. The song, "You've Got To Be Taught" was controversial. It was the early 1960's and racism was being fought openly in the South. The college students insisted that these were adult issues that eluded young children. No, we couldn't possibly have understood the play. "Why don't you ask them yourselves?" my mother challenged. A student turned to me and said, "What do you think the play was about?" I thought for a moment and answered in two words, "Human relationships." The class sat stunned, in silence. My mother was quite proud of me that day. I had demonstrated her point perfectly. Not only had I understood and appreciated the play, I was, in that moment, the perfect child.

As usual, my mother was right. Teachers too often condescend to their students and assume that they can't possibly grasp complex ideas. How can you know if children understand? Why not just ask them? My mother was making these students ask questions that would change their lives as teachers. And I was helping her to do it.

Yet I was left feeling strangely empty. I knew I had performed well. I enjoyed my mother's momentary pride in me as much as I had enjoyed watching the musical, maybe even more. What was missing? Where were *my* questions, *my* feelings and desires? What did *I* want to contribute?

The perspective that these experiences gave me later, as a parent and educator, is hard to explain. I acted out my teacher's faults for a class of student teachers. I showed them what not to do when I was a mere child of eight. The lens through which I viewed education and educators was sharply defined, and my focus continued to grow.

In 1960's USA, there was a great movement to change the world and the way people think. It was happening in the Civil Rights movement, in the hippie movement, in the anti-Vietnam War movement, and it was happening in education. The newly published books that my mother left lying out on the hall table (which I borrowed and read cover to cover) included *How Children Fail*, by John Holt and *Teaching as a Subversive Activity*, by Neil Postman. Dinner conversation spoke of Summerhill, the controversial democratic school in England where kids only took courses if and when they wanted to. I learned about the Open Classroom, an experiment in British education that challenged old ways of thinking and gave students freedom to explore and opportunities to teach each other. NYC schools were being decentralized, and the teacher's union was hailing this as the answer to an overburdened system. Head Start was created, and early education (what we call pre-school today) was finally being provided to the poor in some small way. Free lunches, and then free breakfasts, were offered in school cafeterias to anyone who needed them. Change was afoot.

These were radical ideas that have continued to grow in some places. Today there is a global alternative school movement that includes democratic free schools similar to Summerhill. Jerry Mintz of AERO.org has helped to organize free schools from Brooklyn to India, schools in which the students themselves organize and create their own school system. Various styles of home-schooling, parent-run schools, small private schools, charter schools, and small special ed. schools, also reflect a quiet revolution in education. Students come with such a wide and ever-changing variety of needs and backgrounds that a similar variety of teaching styles and educational philosophies continues to emerge. Sometimes these contradicting theories create a situation that does not work for the child. A student in a loose and unstructured environment may need more structure, for example.

My mother taught me (perhaps through negative example) that your child does not have to take after you. A good educational environment, and a good set of rules or policy in any home or workplace, is created by teamwork, where feedback and suggestions are taken from everyone involved.

The contradictions of all theories meet in addressing the inner needs of the child. It doesn't matter what approach you take towards education, what your philosophy or style is, if you put the child first. The child must feel safe and secure. The child must know that he or she is listened to. The child must feel strong and empowered (not catered to or spoiled, there is a big difference). If these needs are met, you will develop mutual respect.

With all of the strides that have been made in the past fifty years in education, why are our public schools today worse than ever? Are we afraid of the inevitable result of success, the empowerment of our children? Or is our own confusion, perhaps the result of our own education, standing in the way of respecting our children?

Project Muse

On the first day of classes my mother always told a certain story to her college freshmen students. I heard it the first time when I was seven or so, and I heard it again and again. The story came from one of her books on education, I can't remember which, and often students would return, years later, and ask to hear it again. My version of the story goes something like this:

Johnny woke up excited and happy. The sun filled his room with buttery light and the sky was a bright baby blue. He jumped out of bed. Today was his first day of school! He chose his favorite shirt, as yellow as the sun, and hummed all the way through breakfast. On the way to school he felt the gold of the sunlight and he breathed in the green of the grass and he laughed at the day. It was his first day of school! When he arrived at kindergarten his teacher said that it was time to paint. Johnny loved to paint! He dipped his brush in the paint and filled the paper with the blue of the sky and the gold of the sun, the green of the grass and the joy of his first day of school. The teacher came over and looked at the painting. "What's that a picture of?" she asked. Johnny wanted to tell her that it was the golden sunshine and the bright sky and the joy of his first day at school, but none of the words came out. "Look at what Sam is painting," the teacher pointed. "He's painting a helicopter." Johnny looked at the boy next to him and what he was painting. It was black and gray; it was an ugly machine. Johnny tried to paint a helicopter too, but it ruined his painting. It wasn't a painting of the beautiful day anymore. It looked ugly now and he tore it up. Johnny went home sad at the end of the day. He decided that he didn't like school.

Student teachers were so moved by this story that some said it changed their lives. My mother made certain that her students understood the importance of creativity and arts in the curriculum. But the moral of this story is greater than that. Protecting a child's creative voice is the obvious imperative, along with accepting who that child is. In her classes, my mother drummed these ideas into the heads of her students. But at home, as her child, I was not accepted, I was not protected, or encouraged to develop my own creative voice. Instead I felt that my purpose was to make my mother look good, to be obedient to her. I wasn't allowed to relax and be myself.

Filled with ambition, my mother won a national award for a teacher-training program she created called

Project Muse. Her student teachers joined her in the inner city schools of Harlem, where my mom, sometimes
the only white woman visible, fearlessly walked down
the streets, often overladen with materials, bags swinging from her arms. She never encountered a single problem of racial prejudice in a neighborhood most white
folks were afraid to visit. She took me into those classrooms, where I was shocked to see 12-year-old kids in
sixth grade unable to read *One Fish Two Fish*, by Dr.
Seuss, a book I had read independently at age five.

At home I helped prepare educational materials
for these late-reading students. My mother instructed
me to fill a shoebox with everything needed to make a
puppet, and then write a list of simple directions. We
had made puppets at home ever since I could remember.
Every old sock with a hole in the heel had been turned
into some character with button eyes, colored felt had
been wrapped around fingertips, worn-out stockings had
been rolled up and stuffed into cloth heads, dolls had
been made. Even today I love puppets. I put some socks
and buttons and string into a box, and wrote out a list of
steps. The next kit was a kite. Another was for a doll.
I watched my mother take shoeboxes of ideas into that
school in Harlem, with a band of student teachers who
sat down one-on-one with the kids. "If you can read
these directions, then you can make this kite, and we'll
go out to the park and fly it," she told one boy.

My younger sister and I were asked to transcribe
popular songs. We slowed records down on the record
player, repeating the lines over and over again until we
had written them down. My mother used this to teach
children to read. She reasoned that they already knew

the songs from hearing them on the radio. Why not read them as well? After I transcribed "Snoopy and the Red Baron," my mother requested that I do "Ode to Billy Joe". This was a dark, moody song and, in my 12-year-old opinion, about suicide. I questioned my mother's choice, but she was ready for me. Why should everything be sugarcoated for children? Her student teachers worked in inner-city classrooms filled with underprivileged kids who had deeply troubled lives. This was a song she felt certain they would relate to.

Yet at home our personal troubles were not discussed with our parents. If we mentioned any awful events that occurred in our young lives, we were belittled ("You're only a child"), or our story was turned into gossip (every time the phone rang we'd hear our personal tragedy told again), or, worst of all, we were told never to mention it again. I had to be a perfect child. Just as a teacher's unknowing indifference can ruin a child's educational experience, as in little Johnny's story, so my own mother's indifference left an aching void in my life.

At the end of a year spent watching my mother's work in Harlem, she took me to see a show. It was a rock and roll musical production, written, directed and acted by the same students who had been unable to read One Fish Two Fish Red Fish Blue Fish. I could see my mother's hand in their work. She had let them choose slides of her trip to Africa for the backgrounds. A song about a blind man was performed in front of a close-up of an elephant's eye. The achievements of the students impressed everyone, but I could see that my mother was worried. The following year these kids would be back in the same school, in the same system, without my mother's creative approach, without a battery of helpful student teachers working one-on-one. She held back her tears of worry that these kids were ultimately doomed to failure. Project Muse influenced me deeply, and continues to do so.

My First Child

When I became a mother I vowed to protect and nurture the creativity in my child. It was easy to do at home. We became each other's most enthusiastic audience. I will never forget the feeling when I first made my baby really laugh. He must have been two or three months old and I was making faces at him. He laughed so hard at each new face that he fell over. A standing ovation at Carnegie Hall couldn't have given me a bigger thrill.

We cheered our child on at every opportunity. At six weeks he rolled over. He had tucked one leg under his little body for leverage, but couldn't get his arm under his chest to push himself over. We watched his effort, and started rooting for him. "C'mon, you can do it!" we shouted. His efforts doubled. We cheered harder. Finally his hand got into the proper position and he rolled over. We clapped and hoorayed and our little baby gesticulated wildly in the air and giggled with glee. It was easy to be his eager audience when he responded so splendidly.

Education begins at birth. So many of us think of silence and lack of speech as the absence of communication. Nothing could be further from the truth. With the birth of my first child I yearned for him to possess spoken language. I kept thinking that this would open up whole new worlds of communication between us. Yet as soon as he began to speak, I learned how far this notion was from the truth. We began to rely on language to communicate our ideas, and immediately the bond between us lessened. Communication without words is more intense. It was as if we had been reading each other's mind, and stopped when we realized that we could talk instead. I cannot stress enough the value and depth of communication without words. When we are truly in touch with each other, it is not language that is our glue.

At that time I worked as a volunteer for a local family with a son born with cerebral palsy. He was a very intelligent child, and knew a great deal about the human brain. I spent several hours each week at their home, assisting the boy with cross-pattern movements and doing other activities to stimulate brain activity. One day I arrived with a newspaper article to share. The headline proclaimed that brain size could be increased at any age. Studies showed changes in the brains of elderly people who had taken up chess or learned a foreign language. I read the article aloud to this child while we worked on his therapy. He responded, astonished, "You mean everybody doesn't already know that?" He led me to other research about brain damage in children, and the following summer I spent a week studying how to multiply children's intelligence with Glenn Doman at The Institute for the Achievement of Human Potential in Philadelphia.

I started using some of these techniques with my own baby. We made cards that flashed him information (called "bits"), and he begged for more. We introduced the words from his books to him on cards first, and we made books ourselves. Also, we tried to create what Glenn Doman stressed was the most important program of all, a physical program. Every day we took a walk with our baby in a carrier. Every day we chased him, crawling all over the house. We made an obstacle course with chairs and tables and blankets and got down on all fours ourselves to go after him. He loved the chase! We had worried that he wasn't walking soon enough. I calculated the distance on our carpeted floors that Doman had suggested was necessary at this age. It exhausted us to get him to do that much. But as soon as we had succeeded, and lay there panting on the floor, our son calmly stood up and strolled across the room. Victory!

"Bits" of information were cut out of used books and calendars. A series of related pictures was glued to cardboard, and while I flashed them as fast as I possibly could, I would call out what they were. He loved seeing the big dogs. "Greyhound, Husky, Great Dane, Saint Bernard, Belgian Shepherd, Whippet, Collie, Golden Retriever, Rotweiler," I would take a breath. "Those were big dogs." I would choose another pile of ten, perhaps showing paintings by Monet or bones in the foot or vegetables. Doing them as fast as I could, the entire process took minutes. I never showed more than three piles, never more than two or three times a day. He always shouted for more when I put them away. The following day they would be shuffled, with a couple of dogs (or other category) taken out and new ones put in. The idea was not to memorize breeds of dogs, but to understand that there were many different kinds. The associations multiplied in the child's brain.

One day we decided that our son could abandon his high chair and sit with us at the table. This gave him a new perspective on the room, and as he approached his seat he began to gesticulate wildly. "An Go!" he yelled repeatedly. "An Go! An Go!" We couldn't figure out what he was saying. Did he need to go somewhere? But he wasn't leaving, he was staring and pointing and jumping up and down. Suddenly it hit me. He was sitting next to a poster that he hadn't noticed before, a drawing by Vincent Van Gogh! He had been shown "bits" of Van Gogh paintings months ago, but only paintings, no drawings. The association of seeing several works by the same artist had taught him the artist's style, and he had no doubt whatsoever that he was seeing a Van Gogh. I can tell you, we were impressed.

Some of Doman's techniques turned out to be overkill, such as repeating the new words of a book five times a day, when once is usually enough. The expectations that The Institute gave to the family with the cerebral-palsied child were, in the end, unrealistic. They gave them false hope. Yet this was the beginning of my understanding that physical activity is directly related to brain activity.

School and Humiliation

When my child turned four years old he entered preschool. That's when he first asked to be homeschooled. I was stunned. I couldn't believe that he even
knew about homeschooling, but he must have over-
heard a discussion about alternative choices that I had
with other parents from the preschool. I didn't hesitate
to say no. He was an only child then (his brother wasn't
born yet), I had no friends or siblings with children, and
I felt that school would be his only source of friends. Besides, as a child I had gone to school, even though I had
learned everything at home. Growing up, I found my
friends at school, but my parents had provided my academic foundation. I assumed that my son would have
the same experience. I told him that he would get everything that school had to offer, and everything that I had
to offer too. This early dialogue with my son, in retro-
spect, made me come to believe that many parents send
their children to school for social reasons. I also see
how easily I succumbed to societal conformity. If I went
to school, so should he. If everyone goes to school, then
my child will too. Such narrow-minded thinking charac-
terized my own stumbling block.

Soon we encountered a series of difficult situations, eventually at every school my son attended, both public and private. In first grade he complained that he just wasn't normal. "What do you mean?" I asked with concern.

"I'm just not like any other kids. They do whatever people tell them to do. If someone says do this, they do this. If someone says do that, then they do that. But my brain is like a computer and it tells me to do all these wonderful things, and I just don't do whatever anybody tells me." He sighed. "I'm just not normal."

I gazed into my child's sad eyes and wished that more kids were "not normal" like him. I wished that more kids didn't blindly follow orders. I wished that more kids stood up to their elders and said "No!" when they felt like saying no. I thought of all the abused children and all the silent children and all the oppressed children, and I admired my young son for his spirit. Of course, we also told him that he had to listen to his teachers and behave himself in school.

Then one day he came home jubilant. "Guess what?" he shouted gleefully. "I don't have to go back to school anymore!" Naturally, we wanted to know what had happened, and he explained that he had accidentally erased his computer partner's work. He had apologized to her, and she was fine with that, but now the teacher demanded that he apologize to the entire classroom. My son refused. He hadn't wronged the entire room, so why should he have to make a public apology? The teacher told him that until he made such an apology he was no longer welcome in that class. "So you see?" he exulted. "I don't have to go back to school anymore!"

I flashed back to my own memory of public humiliation, a fourth grade experience. We had to wear a white blouse or shirt with dark skirt or pants every Wednesday for assembly day. The principal came through the assembly hall inspecting the kids in our grade, six separate classes. If an entire class was in uniform they got a star, and four stars meant a card for their door. The fourth grade classroom across the hall from us had a window full of cards, and we had none, all because of me. My mother thought I looked terrible in white, and besides those white shirts were impossible to keep clean. She didn't want to waste her money, but relented and bought me one, which was stained and always in the laundry. So nearly every week I showed up out of uniform. One Wednesday my teacher was sitting next to me during assembly when the principal walked by for inspection. She turned to me and whispered, "Don't you just feel like crawling under your seat right now? Don't you just feel so ashamed that you wish you were hiding under your seat?" I said nothing in reply except maybe "mmmm" and stared straight ahead. We returned to class, walking in a straight line in size order, as always. When we entered the room my teacher pulled me aside. As the kids took their seats she said, "Laurie, I want you to tell the entire class what you said to me in assembly." I stared at her and my face turned white. "Go ahead, say what you said to me. Go on." I faced the class and mumbled something about wanting to be under the chair. "What did you say? Speak up!"

"I felt like crawling under the chair," I lied. Only then was I allowed to take my seat.

Public humiliation is cruel, and I felt badly for our son. But we explained to him that even if his teacher were wrong, he would have to comply. Once he had stood up to her and told her no, she had felt pressed to make an ultimatum and use him as an example. Now, in order to protect her supreme authority in the classroom, he would be forced to eat crow. "You don't have to like it, but you do have to do it, and do it politely," we told him. My son felt wronged, and cheated. Not only did he have to face public humiliation, doing exactly what he had refused to do, but he was going to have to continue attending school.

Volunteering in First Grade

In an effort to ease the situation I decided to volunteer in the classroom. The teacher had let me know at the beginning of the year that there was no room for any creative expression in a class of 32 children. I thought that nothing else could have made life harder for my son than an absence of creative expression. I offered to do writing with them. The teacher refused. "Mrs. Spigel, " she said, "what I need is someone to watch the kids during recess. I need three mothers to stand out in the yard with whistles." There was no way I was going to watch children during recess, especially standing guard with a whistle! I explained that what I could do was teach writing to the children. Still, she refused. And I persisted. I said I could come at any time, sit in the back, do whatever she liked, work with whomever she wanted, so long as I could write with the children. Eventually she relented and let me come.

The first day I walked into the back of the room and sat down at a small table. I opened a big pad of paper and held an uncapped marker in my hand. The teacher sent a child over to me. "Work with Harold," she said. "He needs the most help."

I hadn't expected to get a special ed. kid the very

first time I volunteered. Harold sat there and gripped a marker so tightly that I thought he could squeeze it to death. I had assumed I would take dictation, but he wanted to do the writing himself. I drew him out about his interests, and he told me about his big brother. He wanted to say how great his brother was. He thought about his sentence slowly and carefully, and labored over bigger words. "Fun" wasn't good enough, he had to use "exciting" even thought the word was harder to write. Halfway through, when Harold was at a peak of effort, the assistant teacher came over to me and interrupted us. I looked up in surprise. "Harold is slow," she said. "Very, very slooowww. He needs lots of help. He's so sloooww." I practically jumped out of my seat.

"Harold is doing just fine!" I said, my eyes meeting hers. Harold beamed at me as I sat down. He redoubled his efforts, filling the page. Harold would have written anything for me that day, and any day thereafter. I came home seething at the assistant teacher. How dare she interrupt that child just when he was experiencing hard-won achievement, and interrupt him to insult him! I was outraged.

Every Thursday morning I went to this first grade class. As I entered the room and walked to the back, children would cry out, "Oh, take me, take me!" Each child was sent, in turn, and each child wrote.

While I worked, the other kids whispered to each other. "What does she want you to do?"

"She wants you to write about your weekend," answered one kid.

"She wants to know about your dad," answered another. But no two wrote about the same thing. At lunch time, as I would get ready to leave, the teacher and student teacher and paraprofessional assistant would gather to look at the sheets of writing.

"How do you get them to do it?" they asked me. I was at a loss for words. I didn't *get* them to do it. I *let* them do it. I couldn't seem to explain the difference.

At home I told my husband, "It's as if I am sitting there, just sitting there, holding the pen in my hand. And there is an invisible magic door hanging ajar in the air, floating just above the table. Suddenly the child grabs the pen out of my hand and starts writing. It is as if they have just jumped through that open door, while all I did was sit and wait and watch them doing it." You see, I couldn't even explain it to myself. A few months later, when duties at home and work required that I stop volunteering in this classroom, I left a part of my heart there.

My son continued to suffer in first grade. We were told that he was failing math. The news surprised us. This was a child who had discovered odd and even numbers when he was three. He had commented to me about it one day over breakfast. "Mom, did you know that there are some numbers that you can split, and some that you can't?" The past summer, at age five, he had started multiplying on his own. We were on a road trip when he figured out that big trucks, tractor-trailers, had sets of four wheels across, so if you just counted along the side.... Now, in a standardized first grade math curriculum, we were being told he was failing. It was unbelievable. My husband sternly challenged the teacher to let our son complete the entire year's math workbook there on the spot. She pursed her lips. "If he can do that, then why did he say yesterday that four minus one was five?" He was standing right next to us for this conference, and he started to dig his toe into the floor.

"Did you say that four minus one was five?" asked his Dad.

"Well," the toe dug deeper into the linoleum, "well, you see Dad, it's more interesting to give the wrong answer than it is to give the right one." The entire first grade math curriculum was addition and subtraction under ten. My son was bored out of his mind, and getting no attention. But when he gave the wrong answer, especially to a simple question, he got his teacher upset, and that was better than being bored.

In the very final weeks of that year this teacher declared that my son was destined for greatness. "Maybe he'll only cure the common cold, but he'll do something!" she told me. I wondered how you could refer to curing the common cold, something that plagues us all, as "only" doing something. But I kept that thought to myself, and asked his teacher what my son had done for her to respond so positively. She showed me. He had found a mistake in the math workbook. He had brought it to her and showed her where the printed numbers were wrong. In every marking period my son had been rated below average in math. In the final marking period, as a result of his discovery, she brought him up to average.

Private Schooling

The next year we placed our son in a private school. We visited them all first, looking for a place that would meet our kid's intelligence and individuality. We thought we found it, even though it meant driving hours each day, and sacrificing income we didn't have. Entry into this school was via an IQ test, and the kids there were all very smart. To our son this made the biggest difference. He felt he could talk to the other kids.

This particular school claimed to track each child individually. Although there were two classes for each grade, there were as many as eight groups at varying levels. My son went into the highest-level group for math, but a special group had to be created for him and one other child in reading. These two second graders spent their reading sessions with the kindergarten teacher, whom they both disliked. Sometimes, out of frustration, my son would give up and leave the room, seeking a quiet spot to be alone. Then a teacher would have to go after him. The first week a teacher chased him all over the school. The harder my son was pursued the harder he ran. Finally he called out, "If you don't stop chasing me, I'll throw myself out the window." That was the first time we were called into that school, but it wasn't the last. We later found out that it was also the first write-up in my son's file of a suicide attempt.

When we arrived and heard the story we confronted our child. "Did you threaten to throw yourself out the window?" we asked.

"Mom," he said to me, as if I couldn't understand, "all of the windows have bars on them, and they're nailed shut. If they think that I'm going to throw myself out the window, then they're the ones who are crazy!"

This was the beginning of a series of misunderstandings between faculty members and our son. They continued to be alarmed by his behavior, and even to take it personally. As surprising as we found the notion that our son was suicidal, their statement that he had murderous intentions towards his teachers was more alarming. Here's how it happened. One day he was sent to the principal (again, for walking out). The kindergarten teacher was reading a newspaper in the outer office where he had to sit quietly and wait. Bored, he sought her attention, but she ignored him and just turned the pages of the newspaper. He began to make comic pantomimes in the room. He pretended to throw something away, but got no reaction. Then he took the copier fluid, broadly pantomimed unscrewing the cap, and then pretended to pour a drop into the coffee pot. At last, from behind the newspaper, he got a reaction. "Now you've done it. Now you're really in trouble." Immediately she dumped the coffee pot and washed it out. Later they wrote in his file that he had attempted to poison the entire teaching staff.

"But I never actually touched the bottle cap. Honest!" he protested. The school refused to trust or believe my child, who tended to be honest to a fault; they viewed him as potentially destructive and as a liar. And of course now there was no way to prove otherwise.

The response of this expensive private school to nearly every problem was to hire more help. Children had tutors, psychiatrists, educational advisors and assessors. We were told that our child had severe behavioral problems (we wondered why there weren't any at home) and were advised to hire high-priced help. One neurological-psychological test conducted by a psychologist cost us $1200 for three hours. When she was done she told us that we had an erratic genius on our hands who would require a staff of fifty to make him happy. I said, "Thank you very much, but I am enough for this child."

Then my son was expelled from school for walking out of class. He was actually doing what they had taught him to do. Students were told repeatedly that if they felt angry or frustrated they should leave the classroom and go out into the hallway to cool down. My son would feel frustrated, perhaps angry with the teacher, so he would go into the hallway to cool down. But going into the hallway was also a punishment. When kids fought or misbehaved, they were stopped and sent into the hallway. By choosing to go into the hall, and not waiting to be told, my son had taken away their ability to punish him. In hindsight, he believes that the only way they could further punish him was to take away his ability to go into the hallway, and in order to do that they had to expel him.

Two years later we discovered that he had a vision problem. We missed it with the standard vision tests included in his annual physical exams, where he always had 20/20 vision or better. Finally, when he still couldn't read independently at age 11, on the advice of my cousin, an English teacher, we took him to the SUNY College of Optometry in midtown Manhattan for three lengthy testing sessions. It turned out that he couldn't maintain the focus of his eyes for more than fifteen minutes. After that he would get headaches, and was no longer able to see the board at the front of the room, or change focus from the blackboard to the paper on his desk. The headaches had caused him to give up and leave the room. In fact, the vision testers explained every behavioral issue my son had displayed in school. A year and a half later, after diligently practicing eye exercises twice daily, my son's vision was fixed, without glasses.

We also discovered small motor problems that had delayed my son's ability to write. My sister, an occupational therapist, used the term "Lego finger syndrome." This problem also took more than a year of therapy before we saw improvement. Every day my son played with jacks and made balls and figures from clay. He did finger and hand exercises to improve muscle strength and coordination, all based on the work of Mary Benbow (a kinesiologist and occupational therapist) from her introduction in *Loops and Other Groups* (a handwriting cursive curriculum).

We Homeschool

In fourth grade, expelled from school midyear, my son was traumatized. We decided to homeschool. We asked him what he had liked best and least about school. He told us how much he loved library time, when the librarian read wonderful stories out loud while they lay on the floor drawing and coloring. I promised that we would do this every day; I would read aloud while he drew. What he hated most about school was the set timed schedule. Fifteen minutes into a class period he might have mastered the new concept and be done, but he had to suffer 45 more minutes of boredom. Alternately, near the end of the hour he might finally be seriously involved, at a midpoint in his work, when he would be forced to stop. We promised him that we would let him work at his own pace.

He had been frustrated knowing that the other kids could write pages of stuff, when he could barely write a half a page. Even though he knew his ideas were just as good, if not better, he had trouble getting them down on paper. I promised him that he would not be finished with his work until he was proud of it. He would be the judge of when he was done.

We set a goal of a research paper. I asked him to

choose the subject, and he selected the Ice Age. He told me this period fascinated him because it was the very first time man showed his intelligence, the first architecture, the first music, etc. I appreciated his reasoning, and we set out to learn as much about the Ice Age as we could. Again I promised him that we would not be done until he was proud of his work. I said that a research paper (for his age) should be three to five pages long, with at least a five-source bibliography and at least one illustration. I thought that it would take him three months, and we would be done in May or June. We visited the library, the American Museum of Natural History, and, on a road trip, museums in Chicago, Illinois, and Albuquerque, New Mexico. In August his paper was done. It was eight pages long, with three illustrations and an eight-source bibliography (not counting the three museums). And he was proud!

When we decided to homeschool, everyone around us, family and friends, disapproved of our choice. I felt the responsibility of my son's education keenly. Moreover, I compared whatever we did to the top private schools in the country, like the one where he had just been, not the public schools. Every night, instead of my own bedtime reading, I plowed through a stack of teachers' manuals and books on the latest findings in education. I discovered manipulatives in math (at www.etacuisenaire.com) and read about the controversy over inventive spelling in early writing (books by Lucy Calkins). I not only developed my teaching skills at night, but I embraced every opportunity for learning during the day, what I called the "educatable moment." When my son noticed a label "Made in Portugal" and asked, mispronouncing the word, "What is Por-**too**-gal?" I immediately pulled out the atlas and started a conversation that examined political and coastal boundaries of countries in Europe, which led to a discussion on the age of world exploration, which led to a discussion on world trade and communication, from Christopher Columbus to the building of the Suez Canal, all from trying to pronounce a new word.

Planned lessons evolved as they became filled with innovative techniques. My son was delighted with hands-on math manipulatives. He thoroughly enjoyed designing his own inventions and experiments in science. He thrived when his questions and interests were responded to, and soon became an expert in the things he loved, like the scarlet macaw ("fastest bird in the jungle!"), or the Middle Ages (studying feudalism from England to Japan).

We soon realized that the world had become our classroom, and we were no longer limited by our home or by a school. Homeschooling was a misnomer. It was more like world schooling. Science was studied at the American Museum of Natural History or in Central Park. Art courses were taken at museums, local art schools and colleges where he started earning credits in ninth grade. Eventually our budget afforded a math tutor, giving him one-on-one attention that guided him to ever-higher levels. Our son rapidly surpassed his peers who attended the top public and private schools. In fact, they were calling him for homework help!

An enormous hidden benefit in homeschooling was the change in my son's attitude towards adults and authority figures. Up until then every adult in his life had the job of telling him what to do and what not to do. His parents (myself and my husband), had actually been working for the school, making him do all his homework (even if he knew the material and thought it was boring), making him go to bed when he wasn't tired and get up when he was, rushing him through breakfast and racing through maddening traffic to get to school on time, and generally convincing him to obey rules and people whom he clearly did not like or respect. One day, when he was convincing me that he was not from this planet (I saw this as an evolution of the idea that he was "not normal"), he explained that this planet, Earth, was a prison for aliens like him. "You mean that I'm your jailer?" I asked, horrified at the thought.

He hastened to reassure me. "No, not you Mom. It's the teachers. They're the ones."

I thought for a moment. "Well, can't you be sympathetic to them? Can't you feel sorry for them, knowing that they are stuck in the same sick system, being jailers and wardens but still in a prison?"

Without a moment's hesitation, he looked me in the eye and flatly answered, "No."

We were very hard on our son over what had been perceived as willful misbehavior at school. We had done our best to support the teachers, even when we didn't agree with them. We had always told our kids that they needed to do only three things in order to make us happy. These three things are: (1) be kind to others (basically follow the golden rule); (2) take responsibility for your actions, and be accountable; (3) continue your education after high school. Education, we explained, was a lifelong thing. It was that second point that had our son nervous. He had been expelled from school for leaving the classroom, and some of that had to be his responsibility. Only in hindsight, which took us years, did we blame the school entirely. And it was only with hindsight that we realized what a turning point this was for all of us. Our decision to homeschool, made in a state of desperation, turned out to be the best decision of our lives.

Now that we were homeschooling, we regularly took our son with us to work, on our travels, to our place of business. He began to meet other adults whose jobs had nothing to do with telling him what he could or could not do. He observed them doing their work from a new perspective. He was encouraged to meet adults whose work interested him, and interview them (which I would credit as writing and social studies). His resentment towards grownups and authority figures melted away. We found our son speaking to adults in a way that he had never spoken to them before, with genuine interest and obvious respect. Our son's self-confidence and self-esteem increased, and he became socially more sophisticated.

The S Word

When others learned of our homeschooling, the question we were asked most often was how we planned to "socialize" our child. In fact, homeschoolers are asked this question so often that they refer to socialization as the S word. In those early years of homeschooling we found a very small community. In recent years this community has expanded rapidly, and today NYC is saturated with active groups. Where my older son found only a handful of homeschooled kids his age, my younger son found packed classes and groups, and an array of activities that could spin any parent's head. Today the NYC homeschooling community thrives, with cooperative groups and learning centers in many neighborhoods. I see new activities offered to homeschoolers nearly every day. Surprisingly, even in the cultural paradise of NYC, the public misconception that homeschooling occurs only alone at home, as if locked in a closet, still persists.

The idea that children need to be exposed to bullies, insensitive teachers, and a cold, cruel environment, in order to become well-educated, socialized adults, annoys me to no end. It is the exact reverse that is true. As adults, if we find ourselves in an unpleasant work environment, one in which we are taunted, abused, mistreated, undervalued and ignored, should we remain there in order to become more well-seasoned adults? I would advise someone in an untenable work situation to seek another workplace, send out resumes and go on interviews, and search for a place where people are treated kindly, and thanked when they do something right (instead of just being scolded when they do something wrong). Yet countless times I have heard adults, including parents, teachers and principals, advise children to stay put and suffer. They say, "That's the way the world is, and the sooner they learn it the better." It's almost as if they are saying, "I suffered and I survived, so you must do the same." I maintain that no one should meekly submit to a bad environment, especially one they feel powerless to change. By taking control and changing our environment, we empower ourselves and live the lesson that we are truly worth that effort.

When my older son approached adolescence he wanted a bigger social scene and asked to return to school. Our ensuing experience taught us that there are many different types of socialization. Later, when we would get asked how we planned to socialize our children, we would sometimes respond, "Do you mean good socialization or bad?"

The overcrowded classrooms and competitive peer pressure of public middle schools proved to be a seriously unhealthy social environment. My son came home with cuts and bruises along with hurt feelings on a steady basis. He applied to specialized high schools and was accepted, but decided to homeschool when he heard about violence involving the students there. He was already unhappy with the academic offerings at these schools. None offered him the high standards in both math and art that he had come to appreciate. Public schools in NYC were at an all-time low, and he knew by experience that he would find a much more academically challenging environment at home.

Our second son, five years younger than his brother, was given the choice of school or homeschool from the start. He chose school at first, smitten with the very idea of a place where everyone came together just to learn. But by third grade he was singing a different tune. "The kids are starting to get not nice," he complained. He also confided a yearning to be able to go to school in his pajamas.

By that time I was aching to homeschool my youngest, who was heavily involved in extracurricular activities. At age eight he was in the New York City Ballet's production of *The Nutcracker* at Lincoln Center. His third grade teacher demanded that every bit of his homework get done on time, even though he had 26 performances in a five-week period. He did it all, but we had to sacrifice our family time including bedtime story time, which I had always held sacred. As a parent and as an educator I felt that the most important thing that a seven- or eight-year-old could be doing was reading. How could it be right to sacrifice that activity for repetitive test-prep? That year my third-grade son went through three separate three-hour tests in school, all in order to prepare him for the fourth grade exam, which was there to prepare him for the fifth grade exam. He averaged one and a half hours of homework every weekday night, most of it preparation for these tests. I knew that keeping him in public school meant more of the same, and I dreaded it. On top of that, each school was applying pressure. Public school wanted him to quit ballet. Ballet school wanted him to quit his music. We thought it was unfair for an eight-year-old to have to choose. When he asked to homeschool I jumped at the chance. I felt that we were giving up school in order to provide an education, keep the arts alive in his life, and save our sanity and family life in the process.

When my younger son started homeschooling, my older one was trying out public middle school. It wasn't until my older son returned to homeschooling for high school that we homeschooled as a family, all of us together. By then I realized that the age prejudice, all too prevalent in school, had disappeared from their lives. In the homeschooling community parents form groups to create social and educational opportunities for their children. These groups have an age range that spans several years. It is often the topic of interest or level of ability that dictates the group, not their age. My younger son loved chess. At age 12 he was the oldest one in the Homeschoolers' Chess Club. He didn't mind if he played with a six-year-old or an 11-year-old; what mattered most to him was the ability of the player. His favorite opponent was barely seven. The reverse was also true. The younger children didn't idolize the older ones, the way they often do in schools when they are separated by age. Instead, the younger children were confident enough to approach an older child, for a chess game for example. This absence of age prejudice was just the tip of the iceberg. Kids were judging each other on merit and character rather than on appearance, and they judged adults the same way.

At home my sons learned together and separately and they taught each other. Although one was in elementary school and one was in high school, they both chose to learn Latin. They made lists of Latin insults to hurl at each other. Their rivalry displayed itself in music practice too, where they tried to best each other at the perfect piano scale. When they weren't competing, they were proud of each other. The older brother proclaimed he wouldn't be caught dead in tights, but he was exceedingly proud of his dancing younger brother.

Friends and family were again aghast when my older son returned to homeschooling for high school. Now the question was, "But what about college?" Concerns about him applying to college as a homeschooler were needless. Homeschooling turned out to be an asset rather than a liability. Colleges respected these kids as independent learners and wanted them for their diverse backgrounds. When my older son applied to college he was accepted into NYU Film School, one of the most selective programs in the country. He did not have a high school diploma. He did, however, have good test scores, an amazing art portfolio, well-written essays, and a creative resume that only a homeschooler, with the freedom to create his own schedule, could have made. During his high school years my son had designed costumes for a college theater production, studied directing at a local college and directed two plays there, and designed and built a set for an off-off-Broadway play, by himself! With a typical homework load and a standard school schedule he could never have taken advantage of these opportunities. His long list of creative experiences showed the kind of passion and dedication that NYU was looking for.

When it came time for his younger brother to apply to colleges, he, too, knew exactly what he was looking for. Homeschooling had made him an independent learner, self-directed at an early age. He started checking out colleges at age 11, and by the time he reached his mid-teens he knew just what he wanted to ask them. My kids interviewed their colleges before the colleges interviewed them. Each chose to apply to only one school, and both received generous scholarships. I still remember how scared I was of homeschooling at the start. Today, the gratitude expressed by my sons could not be more rewarding.

How to Learn Anything

I believe it is always the parents, and not the school, who chart their children's pathways and guide them to success. How do they do it? By making their children feel safe and secure, by nurturing them in a calm but stimulating environment, by answering their questions and caring for their needs, by cheering them on and offering unending support. But all of this is not enough if the child is not seen, is not heard, is not allowed to be him or herself.

My mother always told me that I could be whatever I wanted to be. I didn't understand until I was an adult that what she really meant was that I could be whatever I wanted only as long as it was on her list. That list turned out to be very short and loaded with impossible goals. Even with my success as a teacher and as a parent, I felt I was a failure in my mother's eyes. Her definition of success for me was probably unattainable. It was this legacy, her feeling unjustifiably ashamed of me, which made me so determined to be proud of every effort my children made. In many ways my mother was right, and yet in many ways she was also wrong. There she taught me what *not* to do.

When I was faced with the prospect of homeschooling, I was terrified. But perhaps I was less terrified than other parents in the same position because I knew that I could become a good educator, and not just because my parents were successful educators at the university level. Although I continued to struggle with not being good enough, with approval issues that all parents and children must at some point struggle with, I knew deep down that I was capable of learning anything.

My mother taught me this when I was in third grade, when she taught me how to sew. But she didn't introduce the task by telling me that she was going to teach me to sew. Instead she told me she was going to teach me how to learn anything!

My mom explained that anyone can learn how to do anything if they can just read and understand the directions. Any skill or knowledge could be acquired if one only knew how to read about it and how to follow the accompanying instructions. She would teach me this through sewing. We would learn how to read directions from a simple pattern; in fact it was a Simplicity pattern, where three pieces of fabric made an A-line skirt.

The pattern contained instructions with a unique vocabulary. My mother explained that every set of instructions has its own language that I would need to become familiar with, and she supplied me with a glossary of sewing terms. I was also told that every project required special equipment. In the sewing store where we bought the pattern and fabric we also bought a few tools with the help of a saleslady who gave good advice. I chose my fabric and the pattern and went home to study the instructions.

Weeks later, when I tried on my finished skirt, I felt so proud! But I didn't feel like I had learned how to sew. Instead, I felt like I had learned how to do *anything*! My mother reinforced this idea by telling me that now I would be able to decipher any set of instructions and arm myself with the proper glossary, tools, and materials, all guaranteed to give me the results I desired in any area or endeavor. I had become a self-sufficient learner! But… could I ever be myself?

With each of my children I worked to bring out their individual strengths. But I also needed to supplement their weaknesses. My youngest son, who loved to think, had trouble reading. I had him tested for vision problems in first grade, wanting to avoid any repetition of the problems his older brother had. But of course no two children are ever the same. This one's vision tested just fine then (until his teens, when he, too, received invaluable vision therapy). Still, he didn't read. He was a daydreamer, and drifted away from every book. It had been necessary to read everything aloud to my firstborn for twelve years. When he was finally able to spend a day with his nose in a book, we all quietly rejoiced. Now was I going to have to read everything aloud to the younger one too?

I had been homeschooling for years, and I thought that it was time for me to give something back to the community. So I started a book club. I reasoned that having other kids in the room might motivate my son to read the books. I spoke to a local librarian and arranged for a group of homeschoolers to meet there once every other week, for 90 minutes. The first half of our time would be spent discussing a book, and in the second

part I would give them a poetry lesson. I had been volunteering as a poetry teacher in the NYC public schools
for many years, and I had dozens, perhaps hundreds, of
poetry lessons up my sleeve. I called the group Laurie's
Literature and Poetry Club. It worked like a charm. My
son started finishing his books, just so that he would be
ready to discuss them with the group. Because I let the
children select the books (we had a democratic voting
process), they would arrive early or stay late to browse
the library shelves and discuss possible nominations.

The kids enjoyed writing poetry. I never pres-
sured anyone and I kept it fun. I taught them that poetry could be about them, and they combed the library's
poetry section. They created self-portrait anthologies,
decorated folders stuffed with poems that reflected a part
of who they were, an idea I took from *Awakening the
Heart,* by Georgia Heard. I also relied on lessons created by Paul B. Janeczko, ideas drawn from *The Grammar
of Fantasy*, by Gianni Rodari, and the groundbreaking
work done with young children chronicled in *Wishes,
Lies and Dreams*, by Kenneth Koch, the great poet and
teacher who inspired me in my youth.

One of the youngest boys in this lit club had trouble speaking and didn't want to write. I had low expectations for him. I understood that he was nervous and
self-protective, so I let him alone. Little did I know that
while he sat in the background of the class, the lessons
were quietly inspiring him.

One day I was at his mother's home with a group
of homeschooling parents, when suddenly her children
announced that they would each read something. The
older daughter went first, with a lovely rhyming verse.

Then her little brother, holding a piece of paper in front of his face while he clenched and unclenched the other hand, recited a long poem. It was about love. "Love is like a train hurtling through the night," he said. "Love is like a storm," while the tears rolled down my cheeks. Afterwards, moved beyond words, his mother embraced me.

I Find Myself

As the group grew older I introduced several different kinds of writing to them. We wrote fairytales, memoirs, short stories, and, personal essays for college applications. I don't remember when other parents started asking me to lead literature discussion groups, and teach poetry and writing to small groups of children. It was a natural transition.

I was already teaching classes and mentoring other parents new to homeschooling, when I witnessed a performance by the 52nd St. Project, a nonprofit organization that produces original theater for children. I saw neighborhood children star in their own two-character mini-musicals, each inspired by the child and written by a professional. I knew in that moment that this was what I wanted to do. I wanted to learn these techniques and give this experience to kids, but I didn't want the adults to write the plays. Pride of authorship, as far as I was concerned, belonged to the children.

Some time later it was my good fortune to study with Daniel Judah Sklar, author of *Playmaking: Children Writing and Performing Their Own Plays*. The techniques used at the 52nd St. Project were adapted from this man's work. I also took educator's workshops at

YoungPlaywrights.org. Daniel recommended the book *Improvisation for the Theater*, by Viola Spolin for use in my classes. In this way I was introduced to improvisation, a precious skill for any writer. I combined and adapted these techniques, and, with Daniel's guidance, became a teacher of playwriting.

Nowhere else have I found a place in which all learning styles seem to meet. In my playwriting classes, children end up working alone, in pairs, in small teams, in large groups. They take direction, give direction, take feedback, give feedback, inspire others, and become inspired by each other. They access their imaginations and they learn to analyze. They brainstorm, write and revise, and revise again. They work spontaneously and thoughtfully, improvising as a team, rehearsing and memorizing. They become a troupe of players who come to trust and rely on each other. Perhaps most importantly of all, they have enormous fun.

Halfway through the course, when the plays are completed, professional actors volunteer to read them. For some students this is the biggest moment they have ever experienced. Their own words are now imbued with life by skilled actors. After the actors take a bow, then it's the playwright's turn. In the next class the students become directors of their plays and actors in each other's, working towards a performance of their own.

A year before my mother died she witnessed my students performing original plays they wrote themselves. I was surprised that she asked to come, since she was usually absorbed in her own work and tended to ignore mine. She sat in the audience and watched these kids, some who had believed they could never write anything, and that they would never want to. I had witnessed their birth as playwrights, and directors, and actors. Now they were making the audience laugh or hold their breath. Afterwards my mother told my husband, "What Laurie did was awesome!" But she never told me.

How much have I learned from my mother? Every day I use the knowledge and experience she gave me. From her I learned not only how to learn, but also how to teach. It was from her emotional neglect, that I learned the importance of giving from an open heart, and developed the willingness to support the varying, often subtle needs of each child. Through my mother's lack of connection, I learned the importance of listening and understanding. Because she could not appreciate me for who I was, I learned to appreciate each child as someone truly unique and special. Because of my mother's constant voicing of my own failures, I enthusiastically applaud my students' every success. I am wowed by their achievements. Strangely, I believe that my mother was the perfect mother for me. Who else could have taught me so much?

Both my parents were great educators. My father started the first graduate department of comparative literature in the City University of NY, and thanks to him I grew up reading plays, discussing literature, and going to the theater. Of course, without my two children I would never have found this path, and never have taken the great adventure that brought me here. It is thanks to my parents and my children that I have become the educator I am today, somehow able to recognize and nurture the unique inner spirit in each of my students. And it is thanks to each student, each class, each turn in the adventure, that I continue to learn and grow.

Part Two

Uncensoring Education

The Uncensored Classroom

In my childhood, major strides were made in modern education. Educators were reading *Teaching as a Subversive Activity*, *The Open Classroom* and *How Children Fail*. Summerhill, a controversial democratic school in England, was in the news. Head Start was a newly founded preschool program for the underprivileged. In NYC, school lunches and even breakfasts were now free to those who needed them. This was all part of a new way of looking at the education of our children. It was astonishing how the obvious had eluded us for so long. After all, how could our children learn if they were hungry? Yet the obvious continues to elude us.

I often meet families with kids who are struggling in school. The parents want their children to succeed, and the children, frustrated, want the same. Yet when I ask a child (of any age) the question: "Can you be yourself in school?" they sometimes respond with a derisive laugh.

"Be myself? Are you kidding?"

Isn't it obvious that our children can't possibly do their best in a situation where they can't even be themselves?

Then I might ask, "Do you feel comfortable and

safe in school?" If the student attends a city public school, the answer is usually no, or silence. Isn't it obvious that if a child doesn't feel relaxed and safe, comfortable enough to express him or herself in the classroom, that this is not a good place for learning?

As a homeschooling parent and educator, I had the opportunity to form small classes. One year I taught creative writing to eight teenagers in the comfort of my home. Their goal was to each write a short story based on a fairy tale. In the very first class the issue of censorship came up. "Can we write anything?" they asked. "Really write anything?" I didn't stop to think. Freedom of expression has always been something very close to my heart, and I knew that I could never censor my students. I told them so immediately. And then I became afraid. What had I done? What terrible things might they say? I hastened to add that I respected them as kind people and I trusted that they would never say anything to hurt each other. I saw each of them solemnly nod in response. Then I added a request. "Please, if someone is reading aloud and they have, shall we say, crossed the line with their language, I just ask that after everyone has reacted, and after all of the laughter and hooting has died down, that we get straight back to work." They all instantly agreed, and there was immediate attention devoted to the activity at hand.

In the end, they learned about what made good writing, whether sex or violence or foul language was gratuitous or germane to the plot or character, and that they could all trust each other. Their parents thanked me for giving their children a safe place where they could learn healthy boundaries for themselves.

I choose to abstain from censoring my younger students as well. When a second or third grader makes jokes about poop, what I privately refer to as bathroom humor, there is no reprimand. If the kids laugh, then I laugh too. While I don't encourage such subject matter, neither do I dismiss it. When a late-writing child in one of my poetry classes finally wrote a poem about his dog's flatulence, it was hailed as a milestone of humor in the class, and proudly published in our final book. The suppression of such an idea would have delayed this child's writing further, and his sense of humor and other forms of expression might have been delayed as well. By encouraging his writing, no matter what the subject, he was also helped to move beyond the immaturity of his expression. What is forbidden often becomes an obsession, while what is encouraged becomes a stepping-stone to the next place.

Censorship is implemented because people are afraid of what will be said. That fear is a declaration that we are not safe, and states that we cannot express ourselves freely. If children must enter a school past guards or through metal detectors, and watch their every step and every word, how can they possibly flourish? To put it another way, when we have to take off our shoes before boarding an airplane, and have baby food and lipstick scrutinized, do we feel safer? We willingly submit to these procedures for safety purposes, but we *feel* like we are at war (which is, sadly, the truth today). What about our children who live their daylight hours of every weekday in our schools? Should they feel like they are at war? Should they be afraid? Or should they be comfortable enough to be allowed to make a mistake, and comfortable enough to express themselves freely, so long as they are not attacking anyone?

What makes a home or classroom or school a place of respect? Many would establish this with a whole lot of rules, creating a conformist, censored environment. But that actually feels like the opposite of respect to the children. When those in authority focus on telling students what to do and what not to do, it's hard to break free of that pattern and listen instead. Respect is ALL about listening. Only when students feel heard do they feel respected. Listening is the essence of the golden rule. Only when the teacher (or parent) really listens to the student, and by that I mean listen not just with their ears but also with their whole mind attuned to them and their whole heart sensing what is behind their words, then and only then will the reverse happen. The student will start to listen to the teacher or parent, in the same way. Respect will flourish without censorship. With just this golden rule being practiced, other rules will melt away. Listen to others as you wish they would listen to you.

Good teaching, like good parenting, is all about listening.

Democracy or Dictatorship

Is your home or classroom a democracy? Ruled by "the people," where everyone has an equal say, and even the rights of the minority are heard? This is indeed rare, and, even where a democratic environment exists, a clear leader may be lacking and needed. When the majority rules, minority rights can become ignored or suppressed. Perhaps your family would best be described as a benevolent dictatorship, with a strong leader at the head, a boss who tries to understand everyone. Yet, even when leadership is generous and kind, it tends to overlook and under-listen as it becomes overburdened. If leadership is established to guard against chaos, instead of to provide inspiration and support, you may find yourself playing the part of a police officer, enforcing the rules of the family or classroom.

So, if you don't want to be a dictator, how do you set rules and abide by them? How do you establish teamwork with a clear leader without bossing everyone around? The answer is by doing it together. Ask each person in the room what they think the rules should be. Create a list of rules together and discuss them until you all agree. I recall a classroom where one student suggested that one important rule should be that nobody gets to do all of the talking, including the teacher! The teacher wrote this down along with all of the other rules, giving the children the respect they deserved. This was, after all, a rule that honored everyone. Sharing responsibility is a major key to success. The boundaries that each individual claims to need will set the path you take. Make your rules together.

As my son and I began each school year we set our priorities. We each took turns, and his educational schedule became a negotiation. I would ask him to list what he felt was most important, and to rank each subject accordingly. I, too, made my list of priorities. One year he announced that he wanted to take two science internships, one at the Hudson River Project and one at The American Museum of Natural History. I agreed that these were worthy ambitions, but, I asked him, where would he find the hours to do both? He looked at his list, and read aloud what had fallen to the bottom. Something had to be at the bottom. It was foreign language. I looked at my list, with English and reading at the top (my personal favorites), and noticed that I, too, had foreign language at the bottom. So, we negotiated. He agreed to go to a language immersion summer camp and spend a few weeks learning nothing but Japanese (something he genuinely wanted to learn), and I agreed to support him in two science internships that year. I was the leader in this discussion and everything was approved by me. But, since I was willing to award my son's first choices with that same priority, he was willing to comply with my request without any resentment. Foreign language study was not eliminated, just postponed.

Similarly, in my lit clubs (groups of ten homeschoolers who meet weekly for an hour or two), I begin by asking students to nominate their choices. They are encouraged to bring in a book to nominate, and I also bring some suggestions. After much discussion, some browsing and reading opening paragraphs aloud, everyone votes. They list several choices, and I tally the votes later, trying to make sure that everyone gets their first or second choice. This becomes our reading list for several months.

Discussions begin by listening to the students. They are each encouraged to pose a question or an idea to the entire group. As they share their likes and dislikes, I introduce the points that I hoped to raise. I am still leading the group, organizing their thoughts around my ideas, establishing an aura of respect and a sense of strength and unity. But I am taking my lead from them. When a student interrupts another and doesn't let them finish, I caution them that I will defend everyone's right to speak, including theirs. They each deserve the same respect. All of my actions as a teacher let them know that they come first.

This student-led approach allows for creative expression and individuality. If I am too busy enforcing rules or keeping to a specific curriculum (as most teachers in today's schools must), then I am no longer offering the children an opportunity to be creative, and those creative moments are often when the greatest learning experiences occur. When a student brings up a marvelous idea that had not yet occurred to any of the rest of us, the whole class will go "Ahhhhhh!" and that's when the best discussion begins.

The Intimate Classroom

When my headstrong, independent, first-born son was entering first grade in a new school, in a new neighborhood, I was anxious about how he would react to the teacher and the class. I knew if he could find his own freedom of expression there, he would probably put up with everything else.

When Parent Orientation Day approached, I thought I might have an opportunity to ask a question, just one. I gave it serious thought. What was the most important thing for me to find out? And how should I word the question? Careful wording can add all sorts of implications, so I worked on it the night before.

My question was, "What are your goals for the personal expression of each child?" By asking the question in this way, I assumed that the teacher had such goals, and she would then be able to answer me quickly and directly. I felt that the attitude of the question was generous and respectful to the teacher, and yet might yield some specific details that I could help my son to focus on.

The answer, though, made my jaw drop. "I'm sorry, Mrs. Spigel," the teacher replied, "but there is no room for personal expression in a class of thirty-two children." Suddenly she added, "Oops. Maybe that didn't come out quite right." But this harried woman had made her point. Thirty-two or thirty-six, or however many the school system allows per class, is simply too much. She often told me, during the year, that my son was taking up more than his 1/32 of the day. Is there really a place where each child needs or receives the exact same amount of attention every day?

What happens when a child who dares to raise his or her hand to ask a question doesn't understand the answer? Will that hand go up again? If the teacher resents the interruption, will that hand continue going up until the child understands the answer to the question? Teachers so often say, "I'm sorry, but there's no time for that question now," or they say that the material will be covered another year (an empty promise). Many children come to the conclusion that they are in school to learn to behave quietly, wait their turn, and please the teacher.

What if the ratio of student to teacher was drastically reversed? What if there was more than one adult for each and every child? The 52nd St. Project, a NYC grant-funded program that makes plays with neighborhood children, does this with enormous success. Children are paired with a writer/actor/director and together the two of them write and perform a short musical play. To assist them are a director and administrative staff, a musical director, and volunteer families who share their vacation homes for intensive experiences. Each child ends up with a staff of supporters and plenty of one-on-one attention. Each child ends up a star.

In my opinion, all public school classes should

be much smaller than they currently are, so that each student can have the attention that they need and deserve. If classes were limited to twenty students or less, and if an assistant teacher were present so that the class could easily be split into two groups, then the learning and teaching process would become much more fruitful. An intimate classroom would result in each child feeling seen and heard.

I would go further to ensure an intimate environment, one in which the teacher understands the child, by having teachers in grades preK - 5 take several days at the beginning of every school year to visit the children in their homes (by appointment, of course). These visits could last a mere 15 minutes. It doesn't take long for a teacher to match the parents' faces to the child's, to note how the child's room is decorated (seeing what the child's interests are), and what the learning environment at home is like. Especially for young children, this might be the first chance for them to meet their teacher, and to do so in familiar surroundings helps to dispel first-day nervousness and begin this important yearlong relationship on the right note. Teachers earn the respect of the families when they open the paths of communication, something that a personal visit allows. Taking the time and trouble to actually make a visit lets the family know that the teacher really cares.

In schools today, the parent is often treated like an unwelcome intruder. I have sat at parent-teacher conferences with a timer ticking away the only five minutes of the term that I am allowed to speak directly with my child's teacher. That doesn't allow even enough time for the standard courtesies that make us all feel welcome, much less the opportunity to delve into any problems and create workable solutions. The parent is regarded as a potential complainer, instead of being treated as a valuable advocate for the child. In truth, a successful education comes out of a partnership between parents (family), teacher, and student. Only when all these individuals successfully come together does the child thrive. A meeting before the school year begins between parent, teacher, and child, offers a unique opportunity that I guarantee will pay off in resulting educational growth. A teacher can grab this moment to ask the parents a few questions about their work, their background and their interests. This information can yield a treasure trove of resources to benefit the entire class (perhaps even the entire school) during the coming school year, and can help build a respectful relationship between teacher and family.

In my small homeschooling classes parents are welcome to observe (we enjoy an appreciative audience) and sometimes they are even invited to participate (such as "Let's play Stump the Parents!" — a game most children love). Classes run for just one or two hours, one day a week, and so there is always time before and after to grab a few moments with the parents or extend my time with the students. In fact, my students have complained when classes fail to go over the planned amount of time, and I consider it the most sincere form of flattery that they arrive early or on time and want to stay late. When there is not enough time to have the conversations we want or need, we do it by e-mail. My students and their parents write to me often, free to ask any question that comes up, or pose a new idea, or request feedback. We all continue to learn from each other. The intimacy we have created extends far beyond the classroom.

Age and Grade Level

When I first started my lit club groups, I allowed the reading level to dictate the age group. In time I had a group of 16 kids ranging in age from seven to 14. I was starting to leave the sessions tired instead of energized, and the kids were starting to misbehave. I began to realize the truth about class size.

Up until that moment I was convinced that it really didn't matter how many kids were in the room if everyone was given equal respect. But after one hour of lit club book discussion, the 16 kids had not had enough time. They were actually switching seats in an effort to be heard and seen. That evening I wondered how many guests I would invite into my home for a book club experience. If we had one hour to discuss a book, would I invite ten or 15 people over? Never! I thought eight would be plenty, and maybe even six would be enough for a rousing discussion. I wanted there to be enough time for everyone to feel comfortable and relaxed, not threatened by the rush to speak, or insulted by someone else stepping on their words. I thought about how long each person would need to feel heard, and I came up with ten as an acceptable limit, eight being preferable.

Not only was the quantity of 16 students posing a

problem in my lit club, but the age range was an obstacle as well. The adolescents, age 12 and up, wanted to discuss mature material, but they didn't want to offend the younger kids. When a girl leaned over to whisper an interpretation of a book to me, while watching over her shoulder to make certain that her younger sibling was out of earshot, I knew there had to be a shift. They were censoring themselves. There were issues they needed to discuss, and they lacked a comfortable, safe arena for the discussion.

I decided to break the group into two parts, with eight children in each, ages seven to 11 in one group, and 12 and up in the other. The mother of an eight-year-old boy complained. She insisted that her gifted son was capable of reading any material. Well, I countered, was he ready to talk about rape? The first book that the older group chose to read was *Lord of the Flies*, and one girl immediately called it a book about rape and murder. She was, of course, right, but those sentiments would have not been openly shared in a room with younger children. So, I asked this mother, was her eight-year-old ready to discuss rape? She blanched and never brought up the subject again.

Age is our best indicator of the varying degrees of emotional maturity in a child. As children approach adolescence and mature, a different kind of expression emerges, both as individuals and as a group. We must encourage our children to express themselves openly, giving them a comfortable zone in which to do it.

Yet "grade level" is not determined by age; it is a mistaken concept, something that is individual and mutable. When I was in fourth grade I raced home jubilant with my test results. Waving the paper above my head I proudly announced to my mother that I was reading at the ninth grade level. My mother sobered me instantly. "No, you're not!" she countered. "You're reading at the fourth grade level *for you!*" That stopped me dead in my tracks, because it was true. Who knew what grade level I would be reading at when I was in ninth grade, or twelfth, or in college? Why, *my own* level, of course!

In a respectful community that interacts with the world, many ages and levels meet. Older children should be encouraged to teach younger ones, elderly residents are often eager to help children from preschoolers to teens, local professionals can actively create internships for teens and young adults. When ages and diverse backgrounds merge together, life is more beneficial and more interesting for everyone. But similar ages also need to gather together. I found the best groups to teach were grades Kindergarten-three, four-six, six-eight, and nine-twelve, approximately ages five-eight, nine-eleven, eleven-thirteen, and fourteen-eighteen. While 13-year-olds are often emotionally ready to join an older group, they are also good leaders for the tweens who are slightly younger.

A Test-Driven System

It was a habit of my mother's to give her freshman college education students a standard sixth grade test on their first day in her class. Would it surprise you to know that most of these college students failed the test? They did just fine on the same exam in sixth grade, but what had they retained? Not much, if you use the same test as a judge. Yet here they were, eager to become teachers who would have to someday administer the same kind of test to their sixth grade students. "What are you really teaching them?" was my mother's obvious question.

The public schools in the United States today are the result of a test-driven system. Funding, promotions, even teachers' salaries, are often dependent on a school's increase in test scores, and on the numbers of enrollment. The pressure on children is evident from the very start. My son, in third grade, wondered aloud one evening if he would be promoted to the fourth grade level. He had been bringing home one and a half hour's worth of homework every night, most of it boring test prep. That year, at age seven, he suffered through three three-hour practice tests at school that were designed to prepare him for the fourth grade test, which had just been instituted citywide in order to prepare kids for their fifth grade level exams. Every teacher was feeling the pressure, as was everyone in the school, right down to my young, shy, bright son, who was lying awake at night wondering if he would make it to the fourth grade.

Tests are really a diagnostic tool, rather than an assessment tool. A diagnosis will pinpoint problems. An assessment will judge situations. Tests tell you what a child does not know, rather than what a child does know. Perhaps what the student does not know is simply how to take this particular test. Or, perhaps a student doesn't know about the Civil War, but is an expert in the European Middle Ages, or capable of repairing an automobile or singing an aria. A test might show a lack of knowledge about the Civil War, while neglecting to discern the presence of knowledge or skill in other areas. Today's over-reliance on testing has led authorities to use them wrongly as assessment tools instead of the diagnostic tools that they really are.

Accurate assessments are based on many things. Colleges will look at an applicant's resume, transcript, portfolio of work, personal interview, and recommendations from teachers and employers, before they look at mere numbers such as test scores.

Our current public educational system, placing undue merit on testing, views education in the opposite way that it should be viewed. There is a strong desire for conformity, for a standardized education that is the same in every classroom throughout the country, a one-size-fits-all curriculum and test. It would be quite comfortable, I suppose, to be able to move from one state to another midyear and enter a strange classroom discovering that they were involved in the very same subject matter and even the very same lesson. It certainly makes the overuse of testing easier, as one single test can be used nationwide. But this very sameness is the death of education. It bores and stifles our children and our teachers, and prevents them from making their own creative and original contributions.

Over-testing results in teaching to the test and prevents experiential learning, often called the only true learning. This perpetuates an artificial and opposite view that all learning must come from books, and that a good education equals high test scores. Over-testing trains the short-term memory, but, as my mother's students proved every year, we do not retain this information. We memorize for the test and then we forget. As my sleepless seven-year-old confirmed, testing results in undue stress. A test-driven system can only fail our children.

Moreover, the one-size-fits-all approach does not encourage children to naturally leap forward, and to develop differently, at different rates, as children do. Every parent of more than one child will tell you that no two children are alike. Often, in fact, they are distinctly different, expressing themselves in entirely different ways. They choose different hobbies, different careers, and different kinds of friends. So, if they are always so different, why should their education be the same?

I recall a parent, earnestly trying to reinforce her statement that she loved her children equally, challenging me to declare the same. "After all," she said, "don't you treat them the same?" I instantly realized that I did not treat my two sons the same way at all. The quiet, shy one, I was constantly trying to bring out of his shell. His older, noisy, impetuous brother was the one whom I always tried to teach restraint. How could I possibly admit to treating them the same if I didn't? In that moment I realized that loving them both equally required that I treat them differently. A good education for every child is a different education for every child!

Child-Inspired Learning and The Three I's

Creating a curriculum based on the interests of the child is easier than one may think. It begins with listening to the child. Listen closely, not just with your ears but with your eyes and your heart. Watch the child to find out what he or she yearns for, and to learn what puts the gleam of excitement in his or her eyes. I would ask the child, and I would ask you, the parent or grand-parent or teacher, this important question: If you could learn anything in the whole wide world, any language (even the ancient ones); any skill; how to make or build anything; how to practice any martial art or dance any step; how to ski or swim or sail; the history of any culture or any place at any time, from ancient Egypt to the Russian space team; the mysteries of any animal; any science, and there are many: astronomy, physics, mathematics, chemistry, medicine and the healing arts, the study of trees or minerals or flowers or birds, the study of ancient bones or weather or the human mind, criminology, zoology, anthropology; mythology; how to play any instrument, or how to paint or weave, or write stories or songs, or make stained glass windows, or build kites, or anything in the whole wide world (because the list is truly endless) -- yes, if you could learn *anything* at all, what would it be?

Give your child three days to answer, but three minutes is all it usually takes. Some parents ask me, what if their child doesn't answer, and I laugh, because a child always has something to say, if you are only willing to listen. I have never had the experience of a child not answering this question. I like to ask it again and again, several times during the year. It's easy for children to answer, but harder for us. Sometimes there is something that we wanted to do or learn as a child, and that desire has yet to be fulfilled. If we ask ourselves this question, and then listen to our hearts, it may lead us to something very interesting.

Perhaps eight-year-old Johnny answers, "I want to learn how to fly an airplane!" and maybe that sets his mom to panic. She shouts, "Pick something else!" She says, "I don't know how to fly, I can't teach you that my-self, and I can't afford the lessons!"

But pause for a moment and realize that a child's interests should always be embraced. It is simply the place from which to start.

For example: reading about airplanes includes memoirs and biographies of famous fliers, and poetry about flying. There is the history of airplanes, which turns out to include the history of war in the 20th centu-ry, a history heavily influenced by the airplane. There is the geography of famous flights. There is the science of flying, Bernoulli's law. You can make a model plane with wings and take it out and see Bernoulli's law in practice, learning and retaining far more than you ever could from reading about it in a book. There is airplane math. How fast can an airplane go? How much fuel does it burn?

How high can it fly? How many passengers will it carry? How much does an airplane weigh? For art the child can draw, build, sculpt, or paint airplanes, and in music and writing he can write songs about flying. If he does his work and behaves himself, then you can treat him to field trips to the control tower of the local airport, or perhaps to observe an airplane mechanic at work. If his interest sustains itself over the years, with his parents' support and encouragement he'll be finding a part-time job when he's old enough and saving up for those flying lessons himself.

I had a shy, quiet student who loved mice. I drew him out in writing classes by encouraging him to write about mice. Eventually he wrote (among other things) an 11-verse poem about superhero mice. But his mother avoided discussing mice with him. Except for this one point, they were an unusually close family. She was, understandably, afraid that he would bring one home, and mice unnerved her. I explained to her that they simply needed to respect each other. Her son must understand that he could never bring home a mouse; but she must support his love of the mouse. I advised her, "Embrace the mouse!" Suddenly her son's reading expanded, as they discovered a whole world of fiction with mouse characters. His science came alive with the evolution and anatomy of the mouse and its place in the biodiversity of planet earth. In one of my classes he made a board game about mice. In the end, his love of learning grew. But the biggest bonus was the change in the relationship between mother and son. Their main source of disagreement had vanished, and occasional moody standoffs were now replaced with a mutual understanding and respect that nurtured their working relationship.

A standard first grade lesson is to learn to recognize that every sentence begins with a capital letter and ends with a period. Realize that what you put in between that capital and that period is entirely up to you! Let it be what interests and motivates you and your child. One parent told me that her daughter yawned over her math workbook, doing less and less work. Then the parent remembered what I had said, and started teaching her horse-loving daughter horse math, and she perked right up!

Traditional education is the three R's, only one of which actually begins with the letter R. (Did an educator really think this up? Reading, writing and 'rithmetic?). Are we supposed to believe that the mainstay of education exists in these three subjects? Focus instead on three I's: your child's Interests, your Interests, and your Immediate environment. It is your child's enthusiasms, and yours too, that will make learning come alive. It is in your immediate environment that learning opportunities will most likely present themselves. Visit the animal clinic around the corner, interview the neighbors, learn to identify the trees on your block. The possibilities that lurk just outside your door are endless.

Sylvia Ashton Warner wrote a book called *Teacher*, which I highly recommend. It tells her story of teaching Maori children in New Zealand. These children, raised in the Maori culture, were suddenly put into British classrooms at age five and expected to succeed. Using the standard reading primers they would fail. But Ms. Warner abandoned those traditional schoolbooks and instead she made her own books using the words of the children.

Each week she asked the children what new words they wanted. Then she wrote them down and gave them those words. The following week, if they didn't know the words, she would take them back because it meant that those were not the right words, they didn't belong to them. And then she would give them new ones.

I did this with my children. They didn't want the simple words in their early readers like cat and bed. They wanted magician and rhinoceros. Once, when my older son was learning French, the younger one came to me asking for help to insult his big brother. "Mom, how do I call him a girl in French?" I thought Mademoiselle would do the trick, and told him so. "And, Mom? How do I call him a moose?" I laughed and told him that mousse was the French word for pudding. As an afterthought I told him a funnier sounding word, pamplemousse, which meant grapefruit. He solemnly asked me to please write down those words. Then he chased his brother around the house, and instead of shouting at him, he simply held up three big word cards that, translated, said, Miss Grapefruit Pudding. Sibling rivalry rarely gave me so much pleasure, and teaching new vocabulary in a new language had never been so easy.

Using your child's environment includes using their own language and their own experiences. When my kids were very little, I made big cardboard books about them. These were simple books, with one sentence per page, and an illustration on the following page. I bound them together inexpensively by punching three holes in the sides and using binder rings. The books were approximately one-foot square, maybe eight or ten pages long. They had titles like We Visit the Zoo, with photos or postcards from our zoo trip for illustrations. These books became our early reading primers.

When my firstborn son was three, his little friends came over to play one day. I thought that he was taking them to his overflowing toy chest, but instead he steered them to the bottom shelf of the corner bookcase to show off these homemade books. His friends were stupefied with jealousy. They didn't have books about themselves at home, made for them by their own loving moms.

The Four Levels of Teaching

When I first started homeschooling, my mother explained a deceptively simple way of looking at education. It is deceptive because, as simple as it is, it explains so much. There are four levels of teaching. At the basest, lowest level of teaching everything comes from the written page. This is the most fundamental level of education, where all knowledge is gained from books. It can get pretty boring turning the page day after day of a well-used curriculum. Even if the information is interesting, the level of learning is limited to what's on the page.

The second level of teaching has the written text accompanied by a visual aid. At this level the educator might use diagrams or a slide show. The lecturer pulls down a map or points to a model or conducts a demonstration. A visual aid awakens the listener, and illustrations help the reader focus and understand. A new way of gaining information is added to the absorption of the text.

The third level of teaching has the students set up the visual aid or display themselves. They conduct the experiment instead of observing the teacher doing it. The American Museum of Natural History Museum workshops and science lab courses are taught this way.

The student enters the laboratory or classroom to find all of the materials they need, along with instructions for conducting the experiment. By conducting the experiment on their own (or building the model, or drawing the map, etc.) another level of learning occurs.

Many people believe that this third level is the highest level of teaching. But there is still a higher level. At the fourth and highest level of teaching *the students come up with the idea* for the experiment or display or project. They conceive and then create their own educational experience. The level of learning has now become wholly experiential, originating from the doer and the thinker, not from the book. Books are now tools, one of many resources that can be used.

I believe that this fourth level is the ultimate goal of every parent and educator. We all hope that we will see our children grow up healthy and strong, able to meet the demands of life in a self-sufficient manner. We yearn to see them ready to embark on an exciting life journey, finding work that fulfills them, with the independence, courage, vision, imagination, and endurance to pursue it. We want them to have their own ideas and forge their own path.

Most of us conceive of this fourth level occurring only when our children are adults, perhaps beginning in university at the graduate school level. But in homeschooling I discovered that this fourth level could be achieved again and again, at every age. Aiming for it had many added benefits. My kids became self-directed learners, and found their direction much earlier in life than I had thought possible.

I made the habit of weekly library visits before my

children could walk. I would choose one
and so would they. My youngest, at age
book on whales and *Aesop's Fables*. Perl
book by Dr. Seuss and a fairy tale, neither
tured his interest. He asked me to read the little book
on whales every night. I thought to myself how nice it
would be when we returned this book and I could read
something else aloud to him. But next week he chose
the same two books. In fact, he took out those books,
on and off, for months. When he chose new books, they
were also on whales, or other versions of fables. Would
it surprise you to know that today, as a young adult, he
studies marine biology and philosophy?

When he was older we planned his educational year together. Since it was his education, he always
got the first choice. "What's most important to you this
year?" I would ask. He usually answered marine biology. (For four years in a row he concentrated on marine
biology. And then in one year he did all of his high
school earth science, chemistry and physics.) So science would go at the top of the list. Then it would be
my turn. Reading was usually my first choice, so that
would go next. And so on. Whatever fell to the bottom
might get postponed until the summer or next year if his
schedule got too full. Even when it came to reading we
would take turns choosing. In eleventh or twelfth grade
we read *Moby Dick* first, his choice, and then moved on
to *One Hundred Years of Solitude*, my choice.

Sometimes a passion sustains itself, but more
often it leads us to the next thing. My older son declared his intention to become a costume designer at
age eleven. I must admit that initially I laughed. But

once he explained his motivation, I took him seriously and challenged him to pursue it. He interviewed a costumer designer, met a wardrobe master who gave him a backstage tour of a Broadway show, and took courses in drawing fashion. That led him to a course in computer graphics and interior design, and the desire to become not just a costume designer, but a set designer as well. At age 16, he was given the amazing opportunity to design and build a set for an off-off Broadway show. One day he came home from his new job shaking his head, and told me how he spent an hour talking the director out of painting the entire set bright orange. "Now I know that I have to become the director," he said sadly. Inwardly I laughed, but this time it was not with doubt but with satisfaction. Directing was a good choice for my son's talents and personality. Soon he was taking directing courses at a local college as a high school student. We toured colleges in the northeast for theater programs where he could study costume design, set design, and directing, all three if he desired. One month before applications for early decision were due, he announced that directing theater no longer interested him. Now it had to be film. This meant a whole new list of colleges needed to be looked at. I wasn't too happy about his sudden change of mind. It struck me that becoming a movie director was a much bigger goal that directing theater, and it scared me. My son reminded that this was his life and he needed to follow his own heart. I agreed. He applied only to NYU Film School and was quickly accepted. Two years later he left NYU. He had decided that directing was no longer his goal. Now he was going to become a writer.

The progression of my son's choices made complete sense. Each thing led him to the next. From costume to set design, to directing plays, to writing stories, in each field he was creating the world of a character. This year he published his first graphic novel, using his artistic and directorial sensibilities to orchestrate the artists and artwork, designing everything from the characters' clothes to the cover of the book, and remaining true to his gift of storytelling.

As our children grow we know only one thing for sure — they are going to change. How they are going to change remains a mystery, but they will surely grow and change. Be unafraid! Dare to empower them to pursue their goal of flying airplanes or directing movies or studying mice, whatever their desire is. It will surely lead them to the right thing.

Focusing on interests, instead of on subjects, allows us to learn in a holistic manner. In fact, it is impossible to separate history from science (from evolution to the influence of discoveries), or math from art (symmetry, perspective, geometry, fractals). Subjects overlap and bleed together. In a single visit to an art museum, a visitor can be exposed to geography, reading, foreign language, history, science, phys. ed. (all that walking), not to mention art. Subjects are not isolated.

Learning how to learn and how to acquire knowledge is far more important than acquiring the knowledge itself. For example, in his book, *Surely You're Joking...,* the Nobel prize-winning physicist, Richard Feynman, tells of a time when he lectured to graduate students on a subject other than his own: biology. He began with anatomical facts, outlining the muscles of a cat. The students interrupted him to say they knew a cat's anatomy by heart. Feynman was stunned at the obvious waste of their time. They had spent two years memorizing the same stuff he had looked up in fifteen minutes. Feynman's ability to research his subject quickly and thoroughly was far more valuable than the students' ability to spend years memorizing facts.

Teaching our children how to learn, and encouraging them to direct themselves, is like helping a starving village grow its own crops in order to feed itself, rather than giving it an overcooked feast that soon vanishes with no more to follow. Instead of subjecting our children to a standardized curriculum, and limiting their learning to the lowest level, we can aspire to a much higher level, and give them an education that is limitless and self-sustaining.

The Creative Classroom

On the wall of Elba Marrero's third grade classroom I noticed this list. She explained that they were all reading *Pinocchio* aloud, the classic by Carlo Collodi, which they compared to the rather crass Disney version. "It's a wonderful book," she confided to me, "with lines like 'What does it take to be a man?' — so much to talk about!" On her blackboard was the list of homework choices. Every child had to do a project on this book, but nowhere on the list did I see the traditional book report. Instead, a child could choose from the following *(italics are my additions as Elba explained the list to me)*:

make a comic book *(of all or part of the story, blank comic book provided)*

make a pop-up book

write a skit and perform it

write a song

write a poem *(or book of poems)*

write a diary of a character

write a travel guide *(of a character)*

create a board game *(blank board game with blank cards and pawns provided)*

make a clay model *(of a character)*

make a diorama *(of a scene in the book)*

create a photo album or scrapbook with captions *(of a character)*

write a correspondence *(between two characters, using letters and envelopes)*

draw maps with legends and captions

any other project you can think of *(one child made chess pieces of the characters using modeling clay)*

A creative classroom encourages the sharing of new and unusual ideas. It is not just about having the arts ever-present. A child who loves chess and chooses to make her "book report" into a chess game, by creating chess pieces of the major characters, will love the process and the finished product. The same level of understanding is required to do any of the projects listed above. But which will enthuse the individual child and provide the deepest experience?

A creative home or classroom provides an environment in which the child's ideas are always welcome, and in which new and unpredictable associations can occur, giving way to innovative thinking. The fish tank in the corner, usually viewed as science, can be surrounded with identification books and encyclopedias on fish, news articles about fish, dictionary definitions of fish, paintings and photographs of fish including fish prints, poetry and stories about fish, found objects that remind us of fish, a daily log noting the behavior and feeding schedule, and so on. While some children may be attracted to scientific research, others may end up writing poetry or songs. All these activities lead the child to a deeper understanding of the subject and allow for an expression of acquired knowledge.

Everyone likes to have a feather in their cap to crown their achievements of the year. A high test score can be that feather, but are those bragging rights enough to make a person feel deeply proud? A traditional research report, perhaps one that merits an A, is another way of earning that feather. But if your heart wasn't in it, how proud will you feel? Creating something that speaks to one's inner self results in something worth saving, worth showing off to the grandparents *and* to the friends, something that expresses the inner voice of the student and so will likely be cherished for a long time to come.

Taking the attitude that all humans are creative beings, not just those who are artistically talented, then a creative classroom is not a luxury, but a necessity. In order for us to solve problems and invent new solutions we must be able to think creatively. This means we must welcome the unpredictable, embrace the unusual, maintain our sense of humor, delight in details, and keep alive our sense of wonder. If we, as educators and parents, practice this attitude, then so will our children and our students. Why stick to a narrow, traditional path that allows only one type of worker to succeed? Is a book report the only acceptable way to show that the student has understood the book? Create your own innovative "project list" and offer your child or your students the option of choosing the way in which they will express their knowledge.

As schools eliminate their arts programs and minimize their phys. ed. programs, children become more lethargic and bored and less creative. It is the creative pursuits, the spirit of play, the practice of fine arts and performing arts, that keep us sharp for the more boring pen and paper tasks, and keep our minds awake and eager to do more. Instead of banishing the arts and minimizing play while maximizing academics and test preparation, the ratio should be reversed. If the arts and physical activities took up the major portion of every day, and academic pursuits were relegated to less than a third of a child's day, I believe children would perform better in all areas.

A creative classroom doesn't just seek to add arts into the curriculum and allow children creative choices in their work. It seeks to stimulate the minds of the children — and their teacher — by opening the door to new and interesting associations and provide an ever-changing atmosphere that reflects the inhabitants. I know of one classroom where children created a blue corner, and brought in whatever blue objects they cared to contribute. Objects were found on route to school, made at home, or brought in from personal collections. Looking at that blue corner, I saw not only the color in a whole new way, but also the objects in a new way, from a robin's egg to a glass jar to a key chain to a postage stamp. Inviting the children to contribute to their space opens the door not only for a creative environment, but also for a creative way of looking at the environment.

Once children have a hand in the building or creation of the classroom space, or of their room at home, perhaps by covering the walls with their favorite poems and postcards, or by building a cardboard city, or by creating an imaginary rain forest, they become vested owners of the space. They continue to interact creatively with that space even when they are not there. The creative process, once begun, cannot be contained.

My children designed their own bedrooms. One turned his into an enchanted rain forest. Painted leaves hung from the ceiling and tree trunks grew in the corners where ceramic parrots or stuffed animals perched. This room was a storyteller's heaven. My other son's room was on its way to becoming an underwater paradise, when he changed his focus to martial arts. He kept the deep blue walls and slightly lighter blue ceiling, but hung a picture of Bruce Lee where a reef might have been, and gave a huge kick bag the central location. He created a room that made him want to work out.

When you pause for a moment at work and imagine what you might cook for dinner, or which color bedspread to buy, or where you would put a piano in your living room, you are being creative in your home even though you are not there. No matter where we are, we continue the work that we have begun. You can function creatively in one place, in this case the home you are vested in, while you exist in another.

I saw a kindergarten classroom where the teacher took her inspiration from her students each year, and together they created a unique indoor space. One year she had a majority of energetic boys, so she chose to concentrate on Arthurian legends. She told more than a hundred stories of the Knights of the Round Table that year, while they studied the Middle Ages and lived inside a homemade castle. The year ended with a medieval feast, complete with jousting, music, and food, created by the kids.

The following year she had an even ratio of boys and girls of a more gentle nature, all animal lovers. They chose to concentrate on enchanted animals. Now, instead of entering the classroom on a drawbridge, you entered by climbing through a large fabric-covered tunnel, an imaginary rabbit hole, and you came out in Wonderland, an enchanted forest built by the children. There they recited William Blake's *Tyger, Tyger*, read *Just So Stories*, by Rudyard Kipling, as well as *The Lion, the Witch and the Wardrobe*, by C. S. Lewis and *The Wind in the Willows*, by Kenneth Grahame. They measured gigantic elephant ears that they cut out of paper and pasted up on the wall next to paper measurements of themselves. Math, science, in fact every subject, was studied in this manner, fact and fiction side by side.

In Richard Lewis's work teaching poetry in NYC schools, he encouraged students to create a rainforest of their own imagining. They took over an entire classroom and made their own unique environment. The children gave tours to older students, naming the imaginary plants and creatures and describing their traits. This rainforest was not scientifically accurate; it had its own science. Teachers noticed that days spent in the imaginary rainforest showed almost no absences, while other days showed a higher rate of absenteeism. The children had created a complete world, taken from their imaginations, which kept them connected to their school.

In each of these cases the students became vested owners of their space. Even when they were away from home or school they remained connected, the same way we all remain connected to our homes no matter where we go. A part of our heart is there.

When learning is a creative process, it is a transformative process. It is the seed of lifelong change, and the pathway to personally satisfying achievement.

Beyond Your Four Walls

Why should schooling happen in a room full of textbooks and desks? Education happens everywhere, often when we least expect it. The trick is to take advantage of our environment and use it to its fullest. Applying your curriculum to your children's daily lives will help them understand and appreciate it in a more complete way. Using your immediate environment to inspire and direct your teaching can provoke and encourage students to see their world differently.

The first reading lesson I taught my children was on the city bus. Whizzing down the streets we passed so many signs: street signs, shop signs, ads, names of buildings. I pointed out a few of the easy ones to recognize, words with double letters. Soon every pizza shop and every coffee shop was recognized with excitement. "Does pizza really have two Zs?" my youngest asked in astonishment. "There are so many pizza shops!" The word "many" is a sign that math is at hand. How many? Paper and pencil appeared in my hand and we began to count. How many pizza shops and how many coffee shops were on our route? Two columns were drawn and counting began. Four strokes down and one across, and soon groups of five marks covered the paper. Now the kids weren't just counting, they were counting by fives, or multiplying. And we didn't just compute, we compared. At home we made a simple bar graph so we could visually see how many more pizzerias there were than coffee shops.

The city bus wasn't the only place that could instantly become a learning and teaching environment. Opportunities were ever-present. The supermarket became a vast resource that I used at every age. I remember propping up my firstborn baby in the shopping cart, his bobbling head hardly able to stay erect, as I wheeled him past the produce section identifying and naming every vegetable in sight. Then we would stand in front of the cheese case and I would babble name after name: gouda, cheddar, manchego, pepper jack, muenster, brie, stilton, chevre, parmesan.... I might have rattled off fifty different names for cheese. My son's eyes grew bright and he seemed to beg for more. As the brain learns to think, it learns to remember information and associate, compare, and consider. Knowing that there are fifty different kinds of cheese makes us wonder if there are that many kinds of apples or fish or shoes or languages (and of course, there are more). As my children grew older, the cheese counter yielded new information. Learning the place of origin for each cheese, we could tour the US and Europe. The spice rack was another amazing opportunity for world travel and history. We learned geography through food.

For a local homeschoolers history and geography fair, my younger son chose to research Madagascar. He arrived not only with facts, but also with a Malagasy Fruit Salad using a recipe he found on the internet. Everyone enjoyed tasting the ingredients that were native to Madagascar, cantaloupe, lichees, and pineapple, and having to guess the secret, invisible ingredient that was Madagascar's main export: vanilla.   Somehow smells and tastes help us to remember and understand.   The Malagasy fruit salad was a big hit at the History Fair.

Science presents itself in the supermarket through nutrition and chemical ingredients.   As I got older, and my children approached their teen years, my eyesight worsened and their vocabulary improved.   They helped me do my marketing by reading the fine print on the labels, and becoming more aware of the nutritional content of foods.   They found out what some of those preservatives and pesticides are and became motivated to shop for organic products.   They helped to plan balanced meals.

Math at the supermarket is everywhere, since everything is numbered and priced.   A child can make certain that the correct change is offered at the checkout counter.   He or she can tally and estimate the contents of the shopping cart and help the family to stay within a budget.   Offer your child his or her own shopping budget for their week's snacks, and watch them price and compare and spend their money with extra care.   How to spend one's own dollars is a more valued lesson than how to spend someone else's.   As a child matures, math becomes about looking at the bigger picture.   How many cans can fit on the shelf in this aisle?   How would you figure that out?   How would you estimate the answer?   How much would it cost to stock a supermarket with food?   How much money does a supermarket take in every day?   How would you find out or estimate?   As you drive home you can ask how much gas is used, how much the toll bridge collects in an hour, and so on.

Supermarkets are also a great place to teach social studies. Truth in print, or a lesson in propaganda, need go no further than the soap or cereal aisle. You can find the many different types of advertising and sales techniques on one box after another. Is this a testimonial (with a celebrity photo), or a bandwagon technique (everyone uses it), or is it a plain folks technique (we're all alike)? Various types of advertising propaganda are always on public display, for scrutiny and comparison, in your daily routine.

It is obvious that the post office is also a place for math, social studies (geography and history) and reading and writing. The post office can be a motivational tool for writing, since letters are mailed and received, and packages are picked up. Reading can feel like an adventure when it comes in the mail. We usually get letters by sending them, so the post office can be a major destination, not just for buying or collecting stamps.

Backyard science, or gardening, can be done in your yard, your window box or terrace, and at your local park. Earth science, life science (biology, botany, ornithology, marine science, etc.), and space science, is often just about looking up, or down, and asking why. Park visits can include nature studies like bird watching or plant identification. Employ standard scientific methods of observation and recording data. Use art (drawing or photography) to record observations. Return at different times of the year and day to record more data. Create your own flower field guide for your local park, or a tree guide for the block you live on.

The corner pet store is a source for more life science, animal and marine biology. A city girl I know became an authority on birds, not from bird watching in the local park, but from visiting the pet store on her corner. Animal shelters want volunteer dog walkers. River and lake conservation groups need interns and volunteers. Local zoos and science museums have internships for teens and educational programs for every age.

Geography and social studies exist in your own neighborhood. Start at the K-1 level by mapping the block you live on, and including the direction of north. Expand by mapping the neighborhood and orienteering as you walk through the park (which way is north? West? South?). Examine the maps of the zoo or the subway or the museum, wherever you happen to be visiting. Grades three and four might draw their own zoo map, middle schoolers a map of the state or country, high schoolers maps of the world. Incorporate earth science by creating topographical maps (either by sculpting the dimensions of the hills and mountains in a 3-D clay map, or by drawing in the elevations in contour lines on paper). Research online for the satellite photo of your own neighborhood and see how your local environment looks when mapped from outer space.

How would you learn the history of your own place? (See the chapter on social studies for more techniques on how to become a historian.) One way is by interviewing the neighbors. Most people came from another place (or their parents or grandparents did) and so they bring some history with them. Have your child conduct an interview with the shopkeeper on the corner, or the local veterinarian, policeman, teacher, or retiree.

Find out their history. Who is the oldest person in the neighborhood? Who has lived on the block for the longest? Interview them about how the block has changed. Grade levels from K-12 can use the interview to learn questioning, planning, writing and organizing answers, sorting data, critical thinking, and good manners too. Conducting a successful interview raises self-esteem, conquers fears, and develops relationships. This is primary source research, obtaining information firsthand. It also builds a sense of community and fosters friendly neighborhood relations.

Your local neighborhood might have a school or college, a business, a retirement home, animal clinic, hospital, museum or other institution that will provide educational opportunities. Call them and ask. Perhaps your child can take a tour of the place, ask questions, seek an internship or apply for a job. Find (or create) a theater group, a sewing circle, a chess or card club, at a local library or retirement home or church or synagogue, outside of your home, using your local resources to connect more deeply with the community.

Your local newspaper can serve as a daily textbook or curriculum guide. I used to joke to my kids that if they could understand everything in *The New York Times* they could teach at a college (and certainly get into one). But you don't have to read the entire newspaper. There is something in the paper for everyone, and knowing what you are interested in makes it easy to choose. We used to share one article a week at the dinner table on Fridays. Each one of us would talk about something we saw in the paper that week, perhaps a new theater or music review, maybe a recipe, a recent sports victory, an interview with a scientist, a new trend in business, a newly restored historical monument, a meaningful editorial, or an archeological find. We found news about our neighborhood, walking tours reviewed, architectural photographs printed, museum and gallery openings listed. From this we created our own walking tours and field trips. We found comics, amusing city anecdotes, political cartoons, weather maps with temperatures around the world, science news, graphs and charts, local eateries and shops, reviews of books and shows not just for adults but also for children. The *NY Times* has a page in their Friday weekend section called "Family Fare" with activities especially for children. Just perusing this page kept us busy all year. (And I didn't even mention reading the headlines and news.)

I recommend using the internet to find out more about opportunities in your hometown. Perhaps just out of sight, or down a road you rarely travel, is a local organization specializing in the ecology or preservation of your area, or a community theater, or an arts organization. When doing a web search be specific. For example: "marine biology internships in southern New Jersey." I am always amazed at what I find.

Be bold in asking people to lead you to other local resources. A favorite saying of mine is: "Shake every tree." Each person can be that tree and you never know when suddenly a precious fruit will drop into your hand. Once I asked people I met by chance at a social gathering for an opportunity for my teenage son to visit the local courts (he was studying American government at the time). I got lucky when I realized I was speaking with a justice at the local criminal court, and he opened many doors for us. My son was able to sit in on a trial and an arraignment, interview the chief justice and her clerk, and follow the legal process on a typical day in the local criminal courthouse.

Shaking every tree, asking everyone we know and meet, connects us to our environment. Using the local environment, and not staying encased in the home or classroom, helps us connect to the world. Finding educational opportunities around every corner — reading on the city bus, math and social studies at the supermarket and post office, US Government in the courthouses, animal science at the pet store and in the park — makes us constantly alert for the next learning opportunity. Our senses are heightened. We look in unexpected places. We look up, at the architecture, at the birds and the trees, looking in the direction most people overlook. We look more closely at each other, through interviews, through "shaking every tree." Using our local community makes our lives more synchronous. Merging your own life and life-style with those of your family members and neighbors increases your connections and your communication. We become interconnected and begin to experience synchronicity in ever-increasing measures. Going beyond your four walls may just be about listening more closely, looking more carefully, being more aware, taking advantage of your environment, and becoming more connected to the world.

Part Three

Teaching the Subjects

A Balancing Act of Feeding the Brain

As funding becomes scarce, schools today are minimizing the fine arts and performing arts, sometimes to the point of eliminating them. Physical education, too, is often pared down to the bone. In its place are hours of boring test prep. Playfulness is often absent from the atmosphere, replaced by conformity, pressure, apprehension, and fear of the test. When a school's funding is based solely on test results, changes like this are sadly inevitable. Yet the desired result, improved academic performance and higher test scores, is an uphill fight when accompanied by a lack of arts and physical programs and an absence of experiential learning.

Brain scientists have proven that cross pattern movement, such as crawling, running, swimming, and brachiating (swinging from an overhead ladder), improves not just physical coordination but brain coordination. The more we develop our physical muscles, the better our brains work. Scientists have also proven that play is a necessary survival skill, important at every age. Play, it turns out, is an activity that activates the brain like nothing else. Employing a playful approach in learning naturally increases the learning. In this instance, schools have their approach backwards. More physical activity rather than less, more creativity rather than less, more playfulness rather than less, would dramatically improve academic skills and test scores.

Replacing creative experiences with repetitive practice only serves to dull young minds. Think for a moment that you are a child struggling to understand and master a skill. As you struggle more, your frustration increases. Is the answer to your problem to heap on extra hours of study? Should playtime now be eliminated, so that your hours of frustration are increased? Of course not! Rather, you should do the reverse. Shorten the hours and shorten the struggle. By creating shorter periods of work, the child is likelier to stay focused. When you set shorter, smaller goals that can be attained with a sense of playfulness a child is far likelier to feel a sense of success. Frustration can kill a child's motivation, but a series of small successes can fuel it.

Music makes us better at math, art makes us smarter in history, physical activity and play make us better at everything. It is the total package that makes a child's mind and body healthy, and keeps his or her spirit alive. The ratio of arts and phys. ed. to academics in schools should be radically reversed. The ideal balance might be two-thirds, or even three-quarters, of a child's day spent in the creative arts and physical pursuits, with the remaining portion devoted to academics.

As we developed our homeschooling routine, we found that we could begin all pencil and paper tasks at breakfast time and be done by lunch, leaving long afternoons for the fun stuff: museums, dance & music classes, science experiments, costume or puppet-making, trips to the park or the skating rink or the hiking trail. Three hours a day for academics turned out to be plenty. (In most schools true learning occupies less than three hours in a day, since much of the day is spent on chaos control and conformity, including rote work and test prep.)

Schools not only have their ratio of time spent on subjects reversed, they have their ratio of students to teachers just as skewed. They use testing in a backwards fashion too, as an assessment tool rather than as a diagnostic tool. They misjudge the amount of time that a child should struggle with a subject, increasing it instead of decreasing it. Yet the largest mistaken perception is the idea that every child deserves the same education. Nothing could be further from the truth.

The No Child Left Behind Act attempted to standardize education further. The idea was that all children would eventually score high on the same test. But children are not standardized, and neither are teachers. No one is at grade level in everything, and most of us will always be ahead in some areas and behind in others. A good education, it turns out, is a different education for everyone, a unique education. Just as each parent knows how different their children are, they also know that a successful outcome for each child is a different outcome for each child.

The sameness of our educational system is the death of education. Teachers are no longer encouraged to get inspiration from their students, or from their environment, or from their own ideas. Standardization has dulled everyone.

It is entirely possible for teachers to allow each of their students to have a different goal, to capitalize on their strengths, and to minimize their weaknesses. I do this in my classes by encouraging students to research what interests them, to write about what moves them, to read what they want to read, to find their own voice and their own style.

I know the luxurious position of a teacher of homeschoolers. I am not faced with an overcrowded room. I have ten or twelve students, a group that I can get to know intimately, and take the time to encourage individually. I am not dictated to by an administration that tells me what curriculum to use. I am not observed and evaluated by a principal and told that I did not cover the mandatory amount of material in the allotted time. I do not have to grade my students and they are never threatened with failure. I have the luxury of allowing my students to get excited about their learning, and the freedom to take my lead from them. I have often abandoned a lesson plan or changed my curriculum because I was inspired by my students to do so. I have the deep satisfaction of students who grow up with me, returning year after year to study with me, instead of experiencing the awful sadness of watching my students go on to deal with bad teachers, seeing my hard work, the student's confidence and empowerment, undone by a bad system.

The ultimate luxury of being a teacher of homeschoolers is that every child has asked to be there. Most teachers cannot even imagine what it would be like to have a class full of children who really want to be there. If I feel that a child is not motivated to be in my class, I advise the parents to choose something else. An ardent reader of nonfiction, for example, might hate taking my fairy tale writing course. In the homeschooling community there is so much to choose from that children can find the learning environment that best suits them. Using child-led learning principles, parents can feel confident encouraging their children to focus on their interests.

How different the energy is in an overcrowded classroom! Overcrowding prevents us from being able to move around freely, limits our play, and restrains our freedom. Lack of personal space makes us feel threatened. Lack of time and attention make us feel ignored and misunderstood. Add to this the unwillingness to be there, since for many children school is like a prison. It's a recipe for restlessness, resentment, and mean-spiritedness amongst the children. When too many people must stay in a room, they feel caged.

It is important to recognize that subjects are not self-contained. For example, science cannot be learned without also learning history, math, art, reading and writing. It is a mistake to think that any school subject can be separated from other fields and types of learning. The arts can and should be integrated into every field of learning, while the physical self is kept moving and alert, not stuck at a desk for hours. This is an integrated, thematic approach, drawing on the interests of teachers and students, and incorporating as many learning and teaching styles and subjects as possible. Using the arts and performance-based learning immediately takes teaching out of that first, most base level, and raises it to the second or third level, with many opportunities for fourth level teaching.

I have titled the following chapters with traditional subjects because this is the view that most people share, but each chapter mentions other subjects, which connect to that focus. As a homeschooling parent, I separated subjects mostly for reporting purposes, and far less often for educational purposes. In the chapter Great Curriculum Ideas, you will find examples of many subjects combined together.

Teachers and parents must also include "non-subjects" that are often crucial to successful learning. There are no classes or curriculum requirements on how to self-prioritize (it is always about the parent's or school's priorities), how to relax, how to get to know someone new, the importance of being true to oneself, and so much more, especially universal spiritual truths such as practicing kindness and compassion. When I was a mere child I often wondered why sign language wasn't a part of every first grade curriculum, because it would eliminate deafness as a disability. Why aren't yoga and tai chi taught when both are keys to fitness and longevity? Why aren't simple eye exercises done daily in grade school (a practice that has nearly eliminated the need for eyeglasses for children in China)? Could these "non-subjects" that defy category be just as important, if not more important, than our traditional curriculum?

Students each need to have a personal creative voice. They each need to work at their own level and pace. They deserve to live and work in a world of mutual respect, and to learn in an active and playful manner. Ideally, they should have constant opportunities to shape the content and style of their own education.

The children in my classes have a great deal of ownership in what goes on. If a student suggests that we do something new, I will probably ask the class to consider it. Their input is very important to me. This is not just because it promotes the kind of respect and team-work that I crave. It is also because it creates a deeper educational experience for everyone in the room, a po-tential for that fourth level. Everyone learns from each other. I look at each child as a resource. I see the par-ents this way too. Everyone is a resource, not just me! I learn so much from them, and this delights all of us. I am never bored when everyone provides input, and my responsibility as a teacher becomes not an overwhelm-ing burden or a tiresome chore, but a shared joy that leaves me elated at the end of the day.

Math

Teaching my children math was daunting to me. One of my worst subjects in school, I was certain that we were doomed to struggle with math as homeschoolers. To top it off, my oldest son was clearly gifted in math. By fourth grade he dazzled me with computations that exceeded my grasp. In fifth grade he asked me, "If pi r squared is the area of a circle, is pi r cubed the area of a sphere?" Until then I had never realized that cubed meant 3D. I had never thought mathematically. My thinking was all in words and images. I had to phone a math teacher to tell my son whether he was right or not.

My husband and I ran a business, and math was part of our lives. When my kids were little, to keep them busy while we worked we gave them tasks. Mostly these were counting tasks. Count this pile of stones, we might say. When they were done, we would ask, how many purple ones are there? And they would sort them and count them again. We showed them how to group piles of five or ten, to make counting easier. I understand now that math is all about counting and measuring in increasingly advanced ways. We had them count and measure everything, just to keep them busy and out of harm's way, and they ended up being very good at math.

But how could I give lessons to a child who was better at the subject than I was? When I explained the algebraic process, he would ask me if he could skip it and just write down the answer. Later I would have to slowly go through the process to check his quickly delivered answer. So I came up with a method called Stump Mom. At the end of a lesson, he was encouraged to create a problem of his own for me to attempt. The only condition to playing Stump Mom was that he had to have the answer first, so that he would know if I got it right or wrong. I must admit that I was rather easy to stump, but it was so much fun for my son that he would try to give me something really hard. This invitation to challenge the adult in charge was a technique I ended up using in my classes.

Math was also a focus of evening family game time. Roll the dice again and again for any board game in order to memorize simple addition. *Yahtzee* is particularly good for mental math computation. Cards teach all kinds of math: war and crazy eights are good matching games for the very young; rummy gets slightly more involved; casino uses addition, and poker uses everything including odds and probability, especially if you allow gambling (try using raisins or peanuts). Backgammon, checkers, and chess use mathematical strategies. Even though math was still a weakness for me, my kids now loved using math whenever they could.

I discovered using manipulatives for every age, not just for the very young, which would have helped me so much when I was a child. Manipulatives are a way of making math tactile and visible. We designed and built structures and measured them. We played with number boards, geoboards, interlocking unifix cubes, and mul-tisided dice. All games use manipulatives. Having my children count stones was using manipulatives.

The kids counted and measured in as many ways as we could think of, using different methods, different units, with varying purposes. They found a whale's weight in metric tons and a mineral's weight in grams. They explored airborne altitudes and oceanic depths and latitudes and longitudes. They measured all of the beds in the house and found their average height. They estimated how many books were on their shelves. They doubled and trebled holiday cookie recipes, and measured the yardage of their Halloween costumes.

On March 14th, we would celebrate Pi Day. We invited other homeschoolers to bring any kind of pie they liked: apple pie, pumpkin pie, chicken potpie, pizza pie (the favorite), any kind of pie! Then, at 1:59, after we each derived the area of our pie, we all ate! March 14th is 3/14, at 1:59 pm those numbers make pi. (Pi is 3.14159...) Kids would bring in charts showing pi to the hundredth place or more, and various other pi decorations. It became an annual Pi Party.

Math was celebrated, and applied to the kids' interests whenever possible. My older son designed stage sets to scale, and his younger brother made graphs of the growth rate of whales. Math found its way into fiction. An imaginary country was created. Characters needed math to get there and math to survive there. Math was evident in the imagined cultural attractions, the rate of the upwards falls and the distance across the gaping gorge. Imaginary currencies were created, numerical codes invented, budgets and itineraries made.

Real-life travel offered abundant opportunities to learn math. On long road trips we got so fed up with our children asking "Are we there yet?" or "How much longer?" that we taught them to check the speedometer for miles per hour and watch for the mile markers so they could figure it out for themselves. Trips, whether for business or pleasure, were planned in advance together, maps examined, distances measured, and borders explored.

My neighbor's 12-year-old daughter came home one day complaining about math class. "Why am I ever going to need to know the radius of a circle?" she demanded to know. She considered math an utter waste of her time. I had to think for a bit before I realized when I actually use the radius of a circle. Whenever I want to take a day trip, or seek a new job, or move to a new home, I look at where I live (or work) and create that circle. For example, I ask myself, how far am I willing to commute to work? Or drive for a day trip? An hour? I mentally consider how far I could travel in one hour by car, by train, by bus, by bicycle or foot, and I come up with a series of circles. I find the edge of the largest circle, and then I think about which direction I want to go in. The next day I told my neighbor to let her daughter plan their next day trip. I suggested that she be given a limited amount of travel time in order to find the radius of her circle. She could be responsible for the budget as well, if her parents gave her the power over how to use the allotted funds. Responsibility creates a vested interest in the outcome. Math gains importance when it is part of a real-life decision-making process.

My children sold lemonade and homemade paper airplanes and used books and toys they no longer wanted. They tallied their lemonade costs to reimburse me for the purchase of their ingredients, and then they determined their profits. They earned an allowance at home for doing chores and completing tasks. That actually took some pressure off of me. I could peek into their bedrooms and say with a shrug, "Oh, I guess you don't care about getting your allowance this week." And the next thing I knew they would be cleaning up their rooms. Allowance was ideally split three ways. One third was for spending, one third was for charity, and one third was to be saved for larger purchases or future plans. Of course, one child chose to save two thirds, and the other spent his too quickly, but they got the idea. Finding a charity that they cared about was a lesson that included reading, science, and social studies.

In high school we found the basis for the required economics course in our daily newspaper. (Economics is listed as social studies in the New York State curriculum, but try understanding this subject without using math.) We had been using the New York Times as a math resource for years: deciphering charts, graphs, weather maps, and reading articles about math. Our own neighborhood became an imaginary setting for an economics challenge. If you were going to open a business in this location, what would it be and why? What would the startup costs be, and the projected annual income? Making a plan like this is only interesting if the student creates the imaginary business he or she wants, in a neighborhood they know firsthand.

Because my sons were both talented in math, and because they had been encouraged to proceed at their own pace, they both studied calculus before their senior year of high school, and then they both chose math electives. They knew they could pursue any kind of math that appealed to them. My older son, who wanted to be a set designer at the time, asked to learn how to read electronic blueprints. His math teacher found a kit at Radio Shack, and he spent six months studying electronics. My younger son, who loved ocean mammals, was already using statistics in his research, and he wanted to learn more.

Amusement park math can include physics. Beach math can include biology. If you look for math you will find it everywhere. Take math away from the boring worksheet and apply it to real life and to your students' interests and imaginations. My kids figured out tips for restaurant checks and taxi fares, built an imaginary currency system, and created their own dice. Dare to bring math out of the boring base level where it has been kept for so long, and raise it to the fourth level, where students will discover it again. Above all, seek to create a foundation of mathematical literacy. It is only with the understanding I now have as an experienced teacher that I realize what all of that early counting and measuring and game playing and lemonade selling led to. These same games, activities, and approaches to math work just as effectively with children who are not mathematically gifted.

Here is a fun geometry lesson for grades 3-6:

The Polygon Alphabet Code

Step 1: Define a line and a line segment (no curves).

Step 2: Define a polygon, an enclosed 2-D shape with three or more sides (a side is a line segment).

Step 3: Find examples of symmetrical and regular polygons (triangles, squares, rectangles, pentagon, hexagon, etc.) and irregular polygons.

Step 4: The student makes 26 different polygons, one for each letter in the alphabet, and colors the polygons.

Step 5: The student writes a message using their own polygon code. They can also put their name on the door of their room in this polygon code.

Science

This was another subject that I seemed to fail at in school. Science, like so many other subjects, demanded memorization with little experiential practice. I thought I would never introduce myself to this study. But I learned that all babies are born scientists. They want to experiment with everything they find and test it. Will it break? What does it taste like? Is it sharp? All of these naturally inquisitive explorations alarm us, especially as new parents. But it was through the eyes of my children that I learned to embrace science.

Begin with the natural world. There is so much to explore! Our daily walks (phys. ed.) became science expeditions. We noted the birds that flew by, the flowers that bloomed, and the trees that graced our block. All children love animals and most will pick a favorite one to study. *Beastly Behaviors*, by J. Benyus, has a checklist of behaviors at the end of each chapter. I copied the checklist and we took it to the zoo, checking off the behaviors we observed, and sketching or photographing the animals. My sons started to stump adults with animal facts. The one who loved ocean mammals made increasingly complicated versions of a board game on whales.

A child in grades 1-3 might do a very simple project on a broad theme, noting the basic traits of an animal, such as: What is a cat? An older child, perhaps in grades 4-8, might choose to focus on one aspect about the animal, such as how cats raise their young or the evolution of the tiger since prehistoric times. A high school age student can narrow the focus further, such as the changes in population and feeding habits of the endangered lynx in Arizona. Animals provide a marvelous opportunity to study geography, since most animals either migrate or are unique to a specific area.

Having a personal relationship with an animal offers a rich learning experience, teaching responsibility, communication skills, and maturity, as well as science. Caring for a pet at home, even if it is a tank of fish, or visiting a stable regularly, or volunteering at a dog shelter to walk dogs, are all possible ventures into science that are fun and rewarding experiences.

I adapted the "scientific method" and simplified it into four steps: (1) decide what you are looking for and what you might expect (form a hypothesis), (2) observe or experiment, (3) record your observations (draw and/or write), (4) compare them to your expectations (hypothesis) and discuss your findings. We learned about electricity by recreating the experiments of Ben Franklin and Thomas Edison. The kitchen and the garden terrace became small laboratories. We used the parks, zoos, and botanical gardens to examine flora and fauna. Lying on your stomach with your face peering into the grass, try examining a square foot of soil for ten minutes or longer. At first you might be bored, but very soon you will notice the amazing amount of life in one square foot of earth.

When experiments were ongoing my younger son got out of bed eagerly. Still in his pajamas, he measured the growth of sprouts or checked the weather gauge to record wind and temperature. I telephoned the local river conservation organization, which took college students and high school seniors as interns. I wanted to know how to prepare my science-loving son for acceptance as an intern years ahead. I explained his passion for whales and ocean creatures. "He already knows that much?" the director asked with surprise. "Bring him over!" At age nine he was working alongside Harvard students, emptying traps, identifying fish, and giving tours to school kids his own age. His writing became a weekly log recording his experiences at this internship. Most zoos, aquariums, and parks have teen intern programs that provide a hands-on science experience. Lakes and forests often have conservation groups that are delighted to partner with schools. We even found an expert who took groups foraging for wild greens in our city parks.

My older son told me that earth science and astronomy were invented for kids. He explained that they answered all of the kid questions, the incessant why questions. Why is the sky blue? Why is the mountain so high? His love of art moved him to draw topographic maps and build models of earth formations. We went mining and collected mineral specimens. We gazed at the stars and attended lectures at the planetarium.

Biology seemed to answer the rest of their incessant questions. Why do bees buzz? Why does corn have silk? I had a stock answer ready for these questions, most of which baffled me. I would say, "Great question!

How do we find out?" I started using post-its, and the questions stuck on our wall until we took them with us to the library or the museum or the computer.

My younger son wanted to do animal dissections. We created a course at another mom's house where six kids went through a series of dissections with a biology teacher. My older son was more squeamish. He used *The Anatomy Coloring Book,* by Lawrence Elson and Wynn Kapit, and learned in a way that made him comfortable, through art.

Science fairs are places where information can be exchanged, games can be played, experiments can be displayed and discoveries shared. A homeschoolers' science fair has proven to be motivation enough to revise a board game or come up with a new informational display or create an invention. It's like having a science party! Science makes fun birthday party experiences too. Children love becoming detectives and sifting through forensic information. I know parents who found everything they needed for their seven-year-old son's party at crimescene.com. They had to remove the bright yellow "crime scene" police tape they had put on their front door for party day because too many neighbors called them in alarm. The party guests examined fingerprints and interviewed all the family members to see who stole the birthday boy's (fictional) money. The guests said it was one of the best parties ever!

Experiments employing scientific method can spring from a simple question or desire to test newfound knowledge. A homeschooling family read in the news about "Mountain Dew mouth," a medical condition commonly found in babies in the Appalachian Mountains of northern Georgia. Mountain Dew, a sugary, highly acidic soda, cheaper than milk or formula, was being put in baby bottles and the baby's teeth would rot and fall out. "Really?" wondered my scientifically curious young friends. "Let's test it!" When I visited their home I was surprised to see a row of glass stoppered bottles each filled with a different liquid: Mountain Dew soda, orange soda, Diet Coke, Pepsi, orange juice, and, for control purposes, water. Each child in the family had donated saved baby teeth to the experiment, and now a tiny tooth sat in the bottom of each bottle. After four weeks, I could see the baby tooth in the Mountain Dew soda was pockmarked, clearly showing signs of deterioration. The baby teeth in the cola sodas had turned a dark brown color. The kids were excited to share their findings at the local science fair that year.

The best science learning is experiential, when a sense of discovery stems from a child's natural curiosity. My sons were encouraged to invent something in 6th grade, but this is a good physics project for any age. Inventions are a way of using science to respond creatively to real needs in your personal life.

Make Your Own Invention

Step 1: Introduce the six simple machines: lever, inclined plane, wheel & axle, screw, wedge, and pulley. Ask your kids to identify examples of simple machines used in their house or bring examples in and identify them in class. Explain which machine is used in each device (for example, the kitchen faucet is a wheel with a screw; a can opener is a lever and a wheel with a wedge-shaped blade). Tell them they can invent something using their knowledge about simple machines.

Step 2: Students spend at least one week noticing the things that bother them and making a list. Inventions are supposed to fill a need. If you make a nifty looking invention that has no purpose, then it will not get used. So first, notice what you need in your life. On my son's list were things like: (1) how to keep my little brother out of my stuff, and (2) how to get another roll of toilet paper when you've run out and there isn't a spare roll within reach. List at least ten needs.

Step 3: Discuss the students' lists and ask them each to select one need that they will address. Students will use art to design their invention by making a sketch of the idea.

Step 4: After the idea has been discussed and the sketch has been viewed, the student makes a list of all the materials they think they will need to make their invention. Each student makes a budget and estimates the costs of the materials.

Step 5: After the budget and purchase list are approved, if it is necessary for the student to refine their design they make another sketch.

Step 6: The student purchases or finds all the materials necessary to build the invention.

Step 7: Students should build their inventions with adult supervision, taking safety precautions. When it is completed, the inventor tests the invention.

Step 8: If the invention requires modifications, the inventor makes another sketch, estimates additional costs and gathers any additional materials. After modifying the invention, the inventor tests it again. Once it works, the inventor should use it, photograph it, and document its use.

Social Studies

Social studies include history and geography and all the social sciences: psychology, anthropology, sociology, linguistics, communication, political science, economics, genealogy, mythology, and folklore. In kindergarten it usually begins with a study of the immediate community. In K-1, children might draw a map of their block and figure out which way is north. In grades 2-3 they might make a map of their neighborhood, in grades 4-5 perhaps a map of their city.

We found that geography and orienteering happened while walking through the park, visiting the zoo, traveling everywhere. Geography is in literature (where authors are from and where stories take place), in science (where animals are from and where they migrate to), and in the imagination. Some of my favorite children's books have fictional maps printed on the flyleaf.

Schools concentrate on history. What really *is* history? Most history textbooks tell the story of conquests from the conqueror's point of view. They are often military histories, going from one war to the next. Schoolbooks in our country seek to promote US patriotism by minimizing our past mistakes and concentrating on our victories. Where primary sources are included, they are often pared down to small snippets. Just as school environments support censorship, so do textbooks.

History should be a fascinating mystery that begs for exploration. My mother, who became a historian at the age of retirement, once asked my six-year-old what he thought research was. "Well, it's when you look up stuff in books, or on the internet, to find out an answer, and then you write it down."

"That's what most people think it is," she replied. "But to me, research is about finding something new. If there isn't something new to discover, why bother?" My mother was hooked on history. She made new connections all the time, and her research consumed her. She taught me how to turn my children into historians by having them use the same methods that real historians use, and which I explain here.

When I teach art history, I begin by defining history and prehistory. When does history actually begin? If it begins with the use of written documentation, then perhaps "history" is limited to the history of the written word, written mostly by educated, aristocratic men. Yet history also includes "prehistory," the life of cave men for example, as well as dinosaurs and the history of our planet before man ever existed.

The Timeline

My kids made their first timeline when they were kindergarten age. In my initial example, I drew a line segment and put a dot at either end, marking one end with the date of my birth and the other with the current date. Using a ruler, I marked ten-year increments to help me place events. Then I wrote in the major events of my life, starting with the most important date, the birth date of the child who was watching me do this. I added all of the other important dates: his little brother's birth, the date of my wedding, the date we moved into our current residence, and anything else that we considered a major life event. When I finished I had completed a timeline of my life. Then my son proceeded to make his first timeline, one that celebrated his life. He marked off each year, and then put in all of the events that he thought were important, with little pictures or words to help tell the story.

We went on to make a timeline of the planet. We used a roll of crepe paper and circled his room over and over again, with human existence appearing finally in black marker on the last half inch. My students love this activity. Four of them stand in the corners of the room. We clap loudly to simulate the big bang and the unwinding of a spool of orange paper begins. One student takes it around the other four, while the rest all call out when they think human beings will appear. As the room gets surrounded with crepe paper I ask them, 'Now?" And they shout, "Yes! Now!" But still the paper slowly unwinds with no sign of a mark. I know of one teacher who did this on a school staircase, and the students climbed eight exhausting flights to find the appearance of human beings at the very end. I like to put a line where dinosaurs existed too, just to give the kids a better perspective on how short the history of human existence really is.

It's easy to make timelines about all sorts of things. I know of a homeschooling family who decided to make one of their house. They visited the Hall of Records and the Dept. of Buildings on-line. They found original architectural plans, traced the ownership of their home, and even found out the occupations and nationalities of the previous owners. This was an exciting family project that lasted for years.

My children learned how to read timelines by making them. They became comfortable with this version of explaining chronological events, ubiquitous in newspapers, magazines, books, museum exhibits, etc. Years later, my kids continued to use timelines to illustrate history and literature reports. My younger son chose to make a lengthy timeline of musical composers (mini-biographies in chronological order) for a seventh grade project, combining his love of music with writing and history. When my older son, in tenth grade, wrote about the book *100 Years of Solitude*, by Gabriel Garcia Marquez, he illustrated his ideas with three timelines that showed the three different time realities of the Buendia family, the city of Macondo, and the outside world.

Primary Sources

A crucial element in making history come to life is the use of primary source material. Any eyewitness account is a primary source. This includes: interviews, letters, diaries, newspaper articles, receipts & invoices, photographs, drawings, political cartoons, scrapbooks, and more. Antiques, museum exhibits, restored homes and reconstructed villages also provide us with primary source material. Using these materials to supplement a textbook or history curriculum turns us into independent researchers, allowing us to come to our own conclusions about the historical facts. If studying ancient Egypt, for example, read the *Egyptian Book of the Dead* (a primary source document), visit the Egyptian galleries at the Metropolitan Museum of Art (they have kids' treasure hunts and free gallery guides) and learn to read hieroglyphics by closely examining tomb paintings and a sarcophagus.

When I was a nine or ten-year-old girl in Brooklyn I came home with a school assignment to write a page about Brooklyn. But in my history book there was only a paragraph. How could I write a whole page based on that? Since this was the pre-internet era, we went to the library. But instead of guiding me to a selection of history books (usually secondary sources written by folks who, we hope, did primary source research), my mother took me to the microfiche and microfilm section. There she introduced me to a major primary source: Brooklyn's first city directory. Today's equivalent of this document is the telephone book, both white and yellow pages. If you ever want to really get to know an area, just read the phone book! I learned about the miller's son who lived down by the ferry, and the widow who lived across the road from the blacksmith, on the same streets I walked on. Then my mother asked to see copies of the earliest newspaper, and we laughed at advertisements for hats and corsets in the 1800s, and gasped at the ferry and boat activity in a time before bridges and tunnels. Headlines about the new automobile proclaimed an end to pollution, referring to animal waste in the streets.

This experience not only changed forever the way I saw history, and the way I felt about Brooklyn, but it also changed the way I looked at libraries and research.

Primary sources became my constant pleasure. When I was interested in the age of exploration, I read the diaries of Columbus and Pigafetta (a member of Magellan's crew). Researching the Revolutionary War, I found myself poring over 1700s political cartoons, American and British, in the picture collection of the New York Public Library (NYPL). Handling actual receipts for slaves and indentured servants, and wills that included human beings in the bequests, found in the archives of the Shomburg Collection (the main NYPL branch in Harlem, on 125th St.) gave me shivers.

Art is a primary source that is often overlooked. When my son was studying the Civil War, I happened to open a book of paintings by Winslow Homer to find that he had documented Civil War encampments. We saw details of uniforms, tents, food, and weapons, all painted by an eyewitness. The study of Greek mythology took us to the ancient Greek vases in the Metropolitan Museum, where several stories were illustrated along with the earliest Olympic games.

The Interview

Interviews are self-created primary sources that can be employed at every grade level. It is a process in which you learn before, during, and after the actual interview. Once an interview subject has been chosen, the student must think of the questions he or she wants to ask. The questions are written down, organized, considered and revised. The student makes an appointment for the interview and must arrive promptly (or perhaps they make a call at an appointed time), prepared to ask questions and take down answers. They need to be spontaneous, allowing new questions to arise from unexpected answers. They should be polite and thank their interview subject at the end. Afterwards it is time to write up the interview. This can include an introduction, perhaps explaining why they chose to interview this person, and an ending with their afterthoughts. The entire process teaches history, social studies, and develops writing skills. More importantly, it raises self-esteem and builds social and communication skills.

Even a five-year-old child can think of questions for a grandparent and conduct an interview. They can consider what they already know about the person and form some thoughtful questions. They can dictate or write the answers, illustrate it with drawings or photographs, and create a historical document in the truest sense. A child can interview a neighbor, family friend, local shopkeeper, dentist or teacher. The information gained from an interview may spark a trip to the library, and possibly a follow-up interview with more questions.

Every year I asked my kids to interview someone of their choosing. Usually they pursued a personal interest, and sought out an individual in a desired profession. Inevitably the question would arise, "How did you get this job?" Answers would include college and higher education. This made my children interested in attending college or university at a very early age. Interviewing people in different professions helped my kids become comfortable speaking to all kinds of adults. They learned to ask interesting questions, ones that led to personal stories instead of yes or no answers. They sharpened their curiosity and let it lead them.

Each person has a unique history to contribute, a special story to tell. Hearing that story firsthand is a completely different experience than reading about it in a book. When the oldest person on your block tells you how the block has changed, or when the local grocer explains that his family survived a war, or when you learn that your friend's father was involved in the Civil Rights Movement, then history suddenly comes alive, and you hearken to it in a whole new way. Becoming the chronicler of that story reminds us that history is constantly in the making and we are a part of it. History is happening right now!

Creating Historical Fiction

Storytelling and anecdotes make any lesson come to life, and historical fiction, both reading it and writing it, is a wonderful tool. After my son read *Johnny Tremaine*, by Esther Forbes, a Revolutionary War novel for children, we walked Boston's Freedom Trail. Seeing famous names on gravestones and original buildings he had just read about made him duly reverent. He stopped, in awe, before the facade of a tavern and whispered to me in hushed tones, "This is where it all began, Mom. This is where the Sons of Liberty hatched their plans!" I didn't have to make that period of history come to life for my son. Esther Forbes had already tackled that job, and now my son had taken over.

When my children chose to do a history project, I invited them to write a traditional report, biography or timeline, create an art object, or write a work of historical fiction. This challenge produced a comic book history of the Revolutionary War, a comic book about the building of the Brooklyn Bridge, a story set during the arrival of guns in Japan told by the son of a samurai, and an illustrated children's book on the Apollo 11 mission to the moon, told from the point of view of an escaped lab mouse.

Creating a historical fiction children's book is a great deal of work. It involves as much research as any serious report, and requires storyboard style planning and lots of illustrations. But it also invites the use of the author's imagination. After the research is done, they must come up with a unique point of view and a fictional character's voice. In the end they will have a book their entire family will cherish, well worth all the hard work. My students have written stories that take place during the transition from Paganism to Christianity in Ireland, during a Playwrights Festival in ancient Greece, during Cleopatra's reign, and more.

History can be the history of anything. In Toronto, Canada, the Bata Museum tells the history of mankind through shoes. One homeschooling mom I know created a history curriculum with a focus on dance. I have seen an amazingly thorough syllabus of American history through music, from early folk songs to hip hop. In his senior year of high school my oldest wanted nothing but theater. So he studied the history of theater, starting with ancient Greek plays, going around the world, reading plays from the Far East, antiapartheid plays of South Africa, and contemporary American theater. He found out who the earliest directors were, what the earliest theaters were like, and what the most modern designs are. Why not study the history of something you love?

Making Classifications

Whenever historians do research they must make classifications. Begin with examples taken from a different source than what you are studying. I like to use the telephone book.

Write down the telephone numbers of every child in the class or take a page from the telephone book and write those numbers down. How many ways can you sort random telephone numbers? Ask the kids for ideas on how to sort them, and then add some of your own. Ideas might include: from smallest number to largest number in numerical order, by name in alphabetical order, by neighborhood, by street, by child's age, by family size, by gender (boys and girls). How many ways are there to sort these numbers? What advantages and disadvantages are there to one method of sorting or to another? Location or neighborhood has obvious uses, but sorting alphabetically makes it easier to find the numbers. The children should realize that there are advantages and disadvantages to each sorting method.

Now take examples from another place. Perhaps examples of art from a period of history you are studying, say five postcards of ancient Roman art, and try to say what is common to each. Make a chart. What is different about the five pictures of ancient art? What is the same? There might be sculpture and mosaics or pottery and paintings, logical categories, but there might be other categories. How many have a picture of a cat, or a soldier or warrior? Are they all from the same location, the same city, the same archeological dig? How many have a utilitarian purpose (a floor or a vase) or are purely decorative (paintings and jewelry, for example). You can use Venn diagrams to sort differences and similarities. The narrower the subject (such as German medieval baskets instead of Roman art), the more specific the results will be.

This is the exact same process that real historians go through every time they discover new material. How to classify something is a matter of intelligent research and choice. There is always more than one way to classify something.

Classifications are also important in science. What distinguishing features separate the families in the animal kingdom and the plant world? Examine how animal and botanical field guides are organized. How are plants or trees classified: by the color of the leaves or flowers, by the texture of the bark or stem, by the trunk's or stalk's width or height, by where it grows? What about by smell, or if they bear edible fruit or seeds?

In the end students should know more than just how to use identification guides or understand classifications in research. They should be making their own field guides about what exists in their own environment, and publishing their own archeological findings and historical research to share with each other.

Living History Theater

There are military reenactments in every state that offer a hands-on experience and a peek into Civil War or Revolutionary War life. Witness a recreation of a memorable event, such as the Lewis & Clark journey, or attend a medieval or Renaissance Fair. Take a family trip to a reconstructed village, like Colonial Williamsburg in Virginia, where you can actively participate in that time period. Find your local historical sites and inquire about their educational programs. At a restored mansion in our local park, a group of homeschooled children spent a day signing up to be Revolutionary war soldiers (or trying to get out of it).

Create your own history fair. Every year a homeschool group in NYC hosts a history fair. They invite their kids to come as a person, place or event. Children arrive, often in costume, prepared with ten clues. Each child takes a turn in front of the room, presenting their clues from most difficult to easiest, pausing after each one to allow the audience to guess. "Who am I?" is the name of this game. As the clues get easier, more and more hands go up, until the historical figure or event or place is guessed. Then the child may continue to answer questions. It is just as much fun being in the audience as being on the stage. Afterwards parents and kids put out historically or geographically related foods to taste, along with other presentations. Food, in fact, is a wonderful resource for history. Knowing what people ate and why and how they cooked it and ate it tells us a lot about them. A year-end history party, with a themed banquet and entertainment, is a wonderful project that an entire class can work on, or a great idea for a birthday party.

Language Arts

In New York State, Language Arts requirements for homeschoolers are divided into four areas for K-8: Reading, English (Grammar, Capitalization, Punctuation, Usage and Vocabulary), Spelling, and Writing. Of course, all of these will occur on a trip to a science museum. Educators and administrators mistakenly divide subjects that naturally go together, and here one subject is divided even further. One former homeschooler who recently entered a specialized (advanced) public high school commented on the fact that she was being taught medieval European history in one class and modern American literature in another. Why not assign Chaucer for literature instead? She knew by experience that reading the literature from the time period she was studying would give her a deeper understanding. Language Arts is one area that can always be combined with another.

Reading

Children should be read to from the moment they can listen. Begin with lullabies and nursery rhymes, fables and fairytales, and over the years grow to chapter books, novels, and plays where each family member takes a part. The earliest independent reading is signs. Exit signs, often in neon red, and stop signs, with their unique color and shape, are easily recognized. The words on doors for push or pull, signs for pizza or toy store, are quickly learned. The next independent reading is usually magazines or comic books. These are also the last to go. When you become too busy to read a novel, do you still read newspapers or magazines? And when you are even too busy for that, aren't you still reading signs? The way reading lessens is the reverse of the way it develops.

Signs and labels can be an amusing way for children to identify things. I posted names on doors, labeled subjects on bookshelves, and kept a stack of word cards on top of the refrigerator. When it came time for dinner, I might announce what we were having by holding up a card that said "spaghetti" and another one that said "salad." Or for lunch I might ask what kind of sandwich they wanted with a choice of words ("egg salad" or "cheese" for example). I distinguished hard-boiled eggs from their uncooked counterparts with penciled drawings on their shells. Mr. and Mrs. H.B. had dialogue bubbles proclaiming how delicious they were, or asking to "Eat me first!"

We subscribed to age-appropriate magazines, allowing the children to choose. We read and reread issues of *Ladybug* or *Zoobooks* or *Kids Discover*. Comics from *Calvin and Hobbes* to *Tintin* found their way into our home. Reading clutter was ever-present.

Every evening (now that we were homeschooling) we took turns reading aloud to each other. In the early years you can discuss a story and its illustrations without any attempts from the child to read. A child of four or five might be asking to read, or pointing to words. This is the time to introduce the words separately. Choose one or two words that are repeated often in the story. Show them separately on cards first. When the child can recognize one or two words, for example "blueberry" and "blueberries," then she is ready to read them whenever they are pointed out in *Blueberries for Sal*, a children's classic by Robert McCloskey. Encourage the child to choose her own books and to ask for the words she wants.

If there is any hesitation in examining words and details, have your child's vision checked. Don't settle for the typically brief eye exam that measures only a few moments of focus at a distance of twenty feet (thus the phrase 20/20 for "perfect" vision). There are many eye muscles at work, and many areas where vision can be faulty: such as peripheral vision, tracking, the speed of changing focus from far to near and back again, depth of field, and more. Find a vision therapist or a college of optometry and get a complete eye exam. After a year of eye therapy, my son was able to enjoy reading for the first time in his life. And without wearing glasses!

Comprehension and pleasure in reading are more important than phonics. Putting too much emphasis on phonics can be misleading to a child. Imagine that a child has never before seen the word "house." If she reads the sentence "Sally lives in a house" as "Sally lives in a horse," then she is not really reading the sentence. But if she reads it as "Sally lives in an apartment," even though "apartment" is far less similar in look and sound to "house" than "horse" is, the child is a true reader, improvising a new word with an appropriate meaning. She is reading the story, not just the words.

Literature discussions at every age should be an exciting exchange of ideas, where meaningful questions are raised. Don't rely on boring reader's guides that pose the same questions and activities over and over (such as, write a new ending to the story). Instead, read what your child is reading, and challenge yourself to find what interests you in the book. Look for it and you will find it. Perhaps there is a reference to another place or time or food or music, or perhaps the writer describes an image particularly well, or perhaps a character captures your sympathies or frightens you. Decide what interests you, and ask your children or your students what interests them. Create the kind of lively, meaningful conversations that keep you thinking long after they are over.

Grammar

Be careful not to overanalyze language, which has a precious and somewhat magical quality, with hidden multiple meanings and uses for so many words. Reading a wide variety of literature is the best way to build vocabulary. Speaking well is your best source for grammar if you write the way you speak. Learning how to proofread, use proofreading marks, and correct your own writing and the writing of others, is a major tool in teaching grammar and learning to revise your own work.

In *The Grammar of Fantasy*, Gianni Rodari writes about a word game called the Fantastic Binomial, which he created to inspire imaginative storytelling. I use the same game to teach parts of speech. First I ask for a volunteer to define a noun: a word for a person, place, thing or idea. We might share a few examples, and note that if you can precede the word with "the," it's a noun. Then everyone writes a noun down secretly on a slip of paper and hands it to me. If I see a noun repeated I might ask them to change it. Then a volunteer is requested to define a verb: an action word, something that a noun might do. Everyone writes one secretly and passes it to me. Now the fun begins as I make unpredictable pairings from their nouns and verbs. Instead of the "bomb explodes," the "unicorn gallops," or the "cat meows," I might say the unicorn explodes and the bomb meows. In response the room dissolves in laughter. I am looking for the happy accident of unlikely images, and I ask the students what kind of story this makes them think of. Why would a bomb meow? By the time we are finished everyone has ideas for stories or poems and most of them are hilarious. Then we play the game again, but this time with a noun and an adjective, or perhaps, eventually, a verb and an adverb. I always begin with a noun and a verb because that is all that is needed to make a sentence. My students beg to play this game. It makes a great warm-up for a writing or poetry lesson.

Spelling

Inventive spelling, or creating made-up spelling based on the word's sounds, can jump-start writing at an early age. I watched a kindergarten classroom use The Take-Out Curriculum, where kids wrote word after word without knowing how to spell, or even how to read. This method is controversial because teachers fear that students will learn to spell words phonetically, instead of correctly.

Spelling is a skill easily learned by a "visual learner." Visual learners are usually avid readers who learn from what they see more easily than from what they hear or do. I was a visual learner, a bookworm who always scored high on spelling tests without ever studying for them. For me, the secret to spelling was (and is) reading.

English is a tough language, drawn from so many others. Every spelling rule is broken, some more than half of the time. Take "i before e" and think of "weird," don't forget "except after c" and think of "fancies." It's enough to drive a spelling student crazy. The only way we learn spelling, if we learn it well, is by individual word recognition. We rely on sheer photographic memory. Every time we think we've misspelled a word we ask ourselves, "Does it look right?" If it doesn't, then we write it over, and over again, until we think it "looks right," and that's the one we choose. It was this realization that led me to the following game.

Take your children's spelling words from their own written vocabulary. Ask the student to look at a page he or she has written and circle or underline the words that might be misspelled. This, in effect, repeats the same self-correction process we go through as adults. Give praise for recognizing misspelled words. If words are selected that are not misspelled, give praise for having spelled those words correctly. If you end up with a short list, add some misspelled words the child failed to notice. This list is the basis for your game. But first let the student erase the misspelled words (if they want to) and rewrite them correctly.

The game is based on a TV show from my childhood called "Concentration." It is a memory, matching game designed for two players.

Spelling Concentration

Step One: To prepare: write down ten (or so) spelling words twice and cut them out. (I do this on my computer where I save time by writing the words once and copying them.) Make sure that the words do not show through the paper, and the backs are blank and identical in size and shape. Mix up the pieces of paper. Place them face down neatly in four rows of five each on a table, to set up your board. Decide who will go first.

Step Two: Player #1 turns over one card, says the word, and then spells it out loud. Then the player turns over a second card, says the word and spells it aloud.

Step Three: If the words are the same, it's a match, and the player takes the two cards and keeps them. Leave two blank spaces in your board (do not rearrange the cards — it's a memory game), and the player goes again. When the words don't match, turn both cards back over and the turn is over. The other player goes next.

Step Four: When all the cards are gone whoever has the most cards (or matches) wins.

Play the game two or three times, for ten or fifteen minutes. Play it again a day or two later, and maybe again at the end of a week, if the student is not bored yet with the same words. At the end of the week you can try quizzing your child on the word list. Most, if not all, of the words will be spelled correctly and easily. It's easy to see why when you count how many times you read the words (slowly and carefully too) each time you play the game.

Handwriting

When a young child draws a stick figure, do we say, "That's wrong! Where's the neck? Where are the feet?" Of course not. Instead we say, "Wow! You're an artist!" But when a letter in the alphabet is lopsided, we can be quick to criticize. Handwriting skill is dependent on hand muscle coordination, and takes time to develop. I recommend starting a child age three to five with a slate and tiny bits of chalk that naturally promote the tripod grip essential to easy writing. This is based on the work of Jan Olsen (*Handwriting Without Tears*). I also like the work of Mary Benbow (*Loops and Other Groups*), especially for cursive, and for her therapeutic hand exercises.

I encourage you to take dictation from your children. Youngsters are able think of stories that are much more advanced than what they are able to write down. Helping children to put their own words and thoughts down on paper is empowering. Eventually they will master the pencil and the computer keyboard. Meanwhile, put their imaginations to work, and present them with their own thrilling words on paper.

Early meaningful handwriting practice can in-clude shopping lists, wish lists (for birthdays or holidays), place cards, labels, greeting cards, and signs (such as, DO NOT DISTURB - MAGICIAN AT WORK created by your child for his or her door).

Writing

For me, poetry is both the beginning and the end of writing. It is the most basic and fundamental sort of writing because a single word can make a poem. Yet at the same time it is the most elegant and eloquent way we have of expressing ourselves through language. Poetry forms both the basis for writing and its pinnacle. It is for babies and the elderly, and for every age in between. It teaches us to master rules and encourages us to break them. It makes us organize our thoughts and compose them and reflect upon them, while it encourages flights of fancy and imaginative freedom.

I believe that all writing, even nonfiction writ-ing, is an outlet for creative, personal expression. Every piece of writing needs a beginning, a middle, and an end. Often, the beginning and the end include personal interests, experiences, and musings. Interviews reflect the interviewer by what questions are asked and how they are phrased. Memoirs are the most personal form of nonfiction writing, and an essential stepping-stone to writing a personal essay for college.

Knowing your target audience is essential for good writing. Take, for example, the typical book report that is usually assigned every month in schools. Perhaps you have read a book that you really want to tell others about. Imagine that there are three people waiting to hear about it. One is your best friend. Another is your grandmother. The third person is a stranger to you, a friend of your parents. Will you talk about this book in the same way to each of these people? Of course not! You might giggle over the more secret parts with your best friend, and then discuss it with your grandmother from a completely different point of view. You might be even more formal with the stranger. In fact, your target audience would define the language, style and content of your words. If there is no target audience at all, how can you be inspired to write?

Including a publishing or bookmaking event at the end of a writing course can validate an author's hard work. It lets the students know just who the target audience is — and it's not the teacher. My students make individual homemade books to contain their poems, stories, interviews, or whatever they have written, and I also publish their writing as a collaborative effort, with a title created by the class, and copies made for everyone. If plays were written, they are performed; poems are read aloud; families and friends admire published books. In the end, the written work becomes a cherished item, not a stack of papers gathering dust. The final publication or presentation becomes a memorable moment, perhaps a turning point in a writer's life.

Assessments

There is no stress like failure. There is no thrill like hard-earned, well-deserved success. When assessments are punitive they create the stress of failure.

Ideally, an assessment tells you where the child is, and what the child needs to do next. Parents and teachers assess their children all day long, in order to communicate well, and in order to help each child take the next step that is right for them. How do we do it? By testing? When you see that your crawling child needs to walk, do you test him first? When your toddler grabs a pencil and scribbles, do you need to test her ability to write? These thoughts are laughable. We don't need to test the child because the child tells us what we need to know. If we know where the child needs to go next, we naturally encourage the process.

The best assessor, in fact the only accurate assessor, is the child. If schools stopped making teachers fill out report cards, and instead asked the children to do this job for themselves, I think you might be surprised. We are usually the harshest judges of ourselves. My intelligent nine-year-old son took six months to do his first research paper so that he would be proud of the finished product. A school would have given him two months to accomplish the same project. If I had asked my son to grade his work in school, he would definitely not have given it an A. He was embarrassed about its quality.

Why do we demand grades or numbers at all? A standardized, punitive system is designed to make people fail. Why have rankings at all if it means that some must fall to the lowest and be labeled that way? Is it a bad thing to still be crawling, almost ready to walk, if you are past the average age of doing so? Isn't the most important thing just to help the child take that first step? Do our assessments serve the purpose of an assessment? Are they needed if our eyes and hearts can see the truth? We could say: "Annie will soon be ready to walk, as she is now crawling across the entire floor!" Or we could say: "Annie's walking is still delayed."

Setting Attainable Goals

Making a child feel proud and capable of achievement is a matter of setting attainable goals. Just as every child is different, every goal needs to be different. Making everyone complete the same curriculum, on the same subject, in the same period of time, with the same goal, is counterproductive to an individual's success.

Setting goals requires understanding where the child is right now, and then choosing a goal that is within reach. If you take your child for a walk every morning for the length of one block, a chart on the front door might state a goal of five blocks. If you increase your walking distance at the rate of one half block per week, in nine or ten weeks you will have attained your goal. Time to celebrate, take a rest, and then start again with a new goal, maybe eight or ten blocks this time.

But how interesting is an additional half a block, or added pages of a more difficult text? Finding the right goal is about finding a meaningful goal. The best goal is one that reflects that fourth level of teaching, a goal that originates from the child. A meaningful goal gives the student a true sense of purpose, a deeper motivation than any increased distance or time or test score can ever give. The personal invention that is made and used, the Halloween costume that is designed and worn, the letter written that results in an interview with someone you yearned to meet, the instrument you build so that you can play it, are all examples of self-created goals, and work that is motivated by a deeper sense of purpose.

Sometimes it becomes necessary to reset your goals. One fall my teenage son chose a hefty science curriculum, using a college freshman level biology text. Midway through the year he sat down to talk to me about the course. He sadly told me that he didn't think he could complete the work in the given time frame. He was doing too many other things, and this biology book was intense. We examined the text and reassessed it, shortening the amount to about 3/4 of the work he had originally planned to complete. This allowed him to focus on other important goals that included performances and internships. At the end of his year he was satisfied that he had accomplished what he set out to do.

I consider it a bonus in my teaching profession that I do not have to fill out report cards for my homeschooled students (in New York State, homeschooling parents are responsible for submitting quarterly reports and a single year-end assessment). I never have to give my children grades or numbers. I never have to rank them. I can easily see who is more gifted and who struggles more. By allowing them each to move and learn at their own pace, they naturally find the right challenge needed to take their next step.

I encourage meaningful goals. In my Make Your Own Board Game class, each child has the goal of creating a game that can be played by the others. This goal naturally motivates them to do the work, including several revisions, with hardly any prompting from me. The goal of a teacher's approval, or a written grade, cannot compare with the goal of having your friends play a game that you created.

When parents ask me to assess their child, I take a look at the child's work, and I interview the child, teacher, and parent. Then I advise the parent about how to personalize the child's educational life and make it more vibrant and exciting, which will naturally increase the child's success. I discuss how the child's struggles might be addressed, and how the child might be empowered. My assessment is always about improvement, and never about grade level.

Take a moment right now for some honest self-reflection. Ask yourself how your work is going. Are you doing an excellent job? Where could you improve more? Do you feel great about your recent achievements? Or do you feel frustrated, unable to rise to the occasion, overwhelmed by your job? How would you rate your own work? How would you rate your workplace? Did you give yourself all A pluses? Or were you hard on yourself?

Our best personal gauge of success is often found

in the eyes of others. It is a teacher's job to give the students an appreciative audience, and to be part of that audience him or herself. A performance at year's end is not what I am talking about. My students discuss each other's work constantly. They are encouraged to be honest and kind, and in this way they learn to accept and give constructive feedback. When opinions diverge and disagreements occur, the students' mutual respect is maintained while their interest is perked. It is boring if everyone always agrees, and much livelier when a diverse group communicates. When the students have a say in the curriculum content, for example, by choosing the book that is being discussed, they approach the class even more eagerly. They think, "This is *my* book that we're talking about today."

Students are motivated to work hard when each next step in their project displays a unique, personal focus, and is well received by a group. The group's excited reception of a student's work can be an enormous thrill. But it is more than that. When we know that others care about our ideas and respect our differing point of view, then we become motivated to develop our ideas in order to share them.

In my opinion the child should always be the assessor, not just of his or her own work, but also of ours. Children should evaluate their teachers, classes and schools, making recommendations for improvements. When we listen to our students they respond naturally by listening to us. Working together, we can set goals that are right for each individual and for the group or school as a whole.

Many homeschooling parents fear that they will

leave something out. They are afraid that their children will grow up with a gaping hole in their education, that some crucial part will have been overlooked. Of course, there is no such thing as a completed education. Education is an ongoing lifelong process, and there are so many things to learn that no one can possibly learn them all. Every educator and every parent knows that you cannot do it all. You have to choose. When you choose, will you make a wrong choice? Will a crucial subject or skill be missed?

The answer to this question is that the child will tell you! If they are bored, increase the level of difficulty and create a more stimulating, more creative environment. If they are overwhelmed, adjust to an easier, calmer, more structured situation. If they are confused, discover the piece of knowledge that is missing. Often they will explain it to you. My older son kept sending me back to the bookstore to return material that he thought was too mundane. He rejected textbook after textbook until I finally brought him in to do his own shopping. Let the students choose their own texts and they will find the right ones. Let the students choose their own fields of study, and they will continue to select what they want and need. When something is missing, they will tell you. If the educational focus remains on how to acquire knowledge, instead of on the amount acquired, then the student will always be able to learn more. If an assessment focuses on the student's personal goals and projects, and ignores the backwards approach of standardized test scores and grades, the child's true knowledge may reveal itself. When the child is heard, there can be no failure, only new roads to potential success.

Great Curriculum Ideas

A curriculum is an educational plan. Planning is always a good thing, and having a Plan B is often essential. Remember that plans are made to be changed, adapted to your own situation and your own students. Here are a few exciting ideas for thematic curricula, aimed at a variety of ages and involving many areas of study. Each allows for a great deal of personal expression. Each concentrates on acquiring learning skills rather than the memorization of knowledge. Each combines several subjects. They have all been inspired by the interests of children and teachers and by our immediate environment. And they are all fun!

The Take-Out Curriculum

This idea is from Pat Martinez, an award-winning kindergarten teacher, who became inspired as she walked to work in busy Manhattan. It is an example of a unique curriculum created not from the teacher's or students' interests (our most reliable sources), but from their immediate environment. Just try to imagine doing this in rural Wyoming! Its beauty is multi-fold: it's fun, it can teach every required subject, and it's absolutely free! Designed for the K-1 level, this is perfect for anyone on the threshold of learning to read and write.

Step 1 (phys. ed. and social studies): Get to know your neighborhood by walking everywhere. Collect take-out menus from as many different restaurants as you can find in a one or two week period. This is a lot of fun!

Step 2 (geography and art): Draw a map of the area or of a given block, showing north. Label some of the restaurants where you got take-out menus.

Step 3 (math): Count your menus. Sort them. How many categories can you find? Examples include: types of food, locations of restaurants, styles of menus. Make a bar graph showing the different types of food. Are there more pizza menus or more Chinese menus? Which category has the most? Which category has the fewest? Compare prices.

Step 4 (language arts and social studies): Examine the menus. Are the restaurant names in different type or colors or languages? Can you read (or sound out) the names? Do the names or foods represent different cultures or countries? How are the menus folded and designed? Are the foods separated into categories of appetizers, entrees and desserts? Meat, fish and vegetables? Pizza and pasta? Are the prices always in a column? What else does each menu say?

Step 5 (writing): Create your own menu with your favorite foods, listing at least two or three items. Encourage inventive spelling if the child is learning the phonetic sounds of letters. This method has kids writing before they can read. You can learn more about word construction at this age by writing "a Mrkn Fud mnu" than by copying down "American Food Menu." Fold the paper however you like. Make up your own restaurant name or menu title, menu format, and list your own made-up prices.

Step 6 (art): Illustrate and color your menu.

Step 7 (science and health): Make a dish from your own menu. Discuss heat convection, temperature for melting cheese (if making pizza or a tuna melt) or boiling water (if making macaroni & cheese), and safety precautions. Or focus on nutrition and how to select a balanced meal from a menu.

Restaurant Curriculum

When Ms. Martinez was transferred from kindergarten to the third grade, she graduated from take-out to restaurants. Her students ate out in different neighborhoods, mapping their routes through Manhattan. They studied the history and geography of Korea and ate Korean-style barbecue in Koreatown. Anticipating Martin Luther King Jr. Day they ate real soul food at a church on 125th St. in Harlem, celebrating African-American history in more ways than one. They ate at a popular pizzeria, where kids often stopped after school, and discussed immigration and family recipes with the Italian owners.

Students always came prepared with a list of questions for the owner or manager at every destination, ranging in topics from the history of the food to restaurant security. They wrote up their interviews afterwards (organizing research from a primary source), and compared them. They drew pictures of storefronts in each neighborhood, appreciating the various cultures. They polled their taste-testing opinions and graphed the results. A cost analysis and nutritional analysis of the meals would fulfill additional goals in math, science and health. Walking outdoors to and

from the restaurants added a relaxing physical component. Sadly, this third-grade curriculum is not free,
but it is delicious!

Zoo Curriculum

This curriculum practically teaches itself, since most children love going to the zoo. Also, it includes every single subject required by the Dept. of Education in New York State. It was designed for third grade, but can be easily adapted for preK-12.

Social Studies: In NYC there is a zoo in every one of the five boroughs. Taking a trip to each zoo is a lesson in the geography of our city. Each child can highlight the routes taken on their own subway map. Each zoo has a map of the zoo, and each child can trace the paths they take. Cultural differences in each neighborhood can be discussed. The different ways each zoo is designed can be compared. Geography can include learning the country of origin of various zoo animals.

Math: Children can compute and compare the distance to each zoo, as well as the size (acreage) of each zoo. Children can create an imaginary zoo and make their own fictional map, with a map legend and a distance scale. Statistics can be obtained from zoos. How much are the elephants fed every day? How much does a full-grown adult elephant weigh? How much does a baby elephant weigh? How many employees work at the zoo? How many people attend in a year? What is their busiest day? Zoo math can be as simple or as complicated as you like. Circle graphs can be made of each zoo showing how many different types of animals they have. What percentage are water animals? What percentage are birds? A bar graph could compare the number of big cats at every zoo. Similarly, you could analyze how a zoo spends its income, or how far away their animals come from, or how long the footpaths are.

Language Arts: Before you go to the zoo, read about the animals you will see. Children can pick their favorite animal to read about and choose their books individually. They can research the animal's behavior and write a list of five behaviors that they might be able to observe. These can be compiled into a collaborative checklist that each child can take to the zoo. Afterwards they can continue to research their chosen animal, and do a project (see a list of suggestions in the chapter The Creative Classroom). They can also make a collaborative book, each contributing at least one page to a publication. The children could choose the focus of such a book, which might contain scientific data, myths, fictional stories, or poems about animals that include some scientific facts.

Science: Biology and animal behavior is a natural part of this curriculum. Scientific method is involved in the study and observation of each zoo animal. Children could focus on a particular aspect of their animal, such as the animal's anatomy, or its evolution, or how it raises its young, or whether it is endangered today. Science questions can be prepared to ask a zookeeper, such as what an animal eats, or what they do if an animal gets sick, or if they have ever witnessed a birth.

Art: Drawings or photographs or paintings can be made with written captions and compiled into a collaborative zoo scrapbook. Clay animals can be sculpted to make a 3D imaginary zoo. Animal masks can be made and a play can be written and performed. Paintings and sculptures of animals by well-known artists can be examined and reproductions can be displayed.

Music: Songs can be written; a play or skit can be musicalized. Music inspired by animal stories can be listened to, such as *Carnival of the Animals*, by Saint-Saens, or *Peter and the Wolf*, by Prokovief. (There are beautifully illustrated books about both.) Children can spontaneously create music that describes their chosen animal.

Phys. ed.: Dance movements, too, can be created by the children to describe the animals. But you don't need to add a special phys. ed component. Walking through every zoo, this is one curriculum that keeps you moving on your feet!

The Herbal Curriculum

In 1994 Elba Marrero won the Disney Teacher of the Year award for creating this curriculum, designed for special ed. 5th graders who were functioning on a 2nd grade level. As a result of this course, children who had been struggling in every subject blossomed as scientists, poets and entrepreneurs. They manufactured and sold their own sachets and pot pourris, and called themselves "Mini-Greenhouse Herb Factory Gardeners." The beauty of this interdisciplinary curriculum is that it is also a multi-sensory learning experience.

> Step 1: Define an herb. Invite students to bring in samples of herbs found at home. Discuss how these herbs are used. If they are used in a recipe, bring in the recipe to share. Children may return home to interview a parent or a grandparent, and bring in new information to the next class. If enough recipes are brought in they can be compiled into a class herbal cookbook.

> Step 2: Find out what herbs are sold at local markets and what they are commonly used

for. How many countries do these herbs originate from? Read folktales about herbs. Trace their history and migration. Relate the use of herbs to any other area you are studying (how they were used in ancient Greece or the European Middle Ages, for example). Interview a local pharmacist to find out which medicines come from herbs.

Step 3: Visit an herb garden and a greenhouse, possibly your local botanical gardens. Smell the flowers. Rub the herb leaves between your fingers to smell them. Sit in the garden and write poetry and draw while listening to music such as Vivaldi's *The Four Seasons*. Read literature, such as *The Secret Garden*, by Frances Hodgson Burnett, which is a story about transformation. Read some Native American myths about transformation. Gardening, from planting seeds to harvesting, is the study of transformation and growth. Design and write about your own secret garden and its transformation. At the end of this course, write about how you have changed or transformed during the year, or during your life.

Step 4: Plan your own mini-greenhouse herb garden for scent. Research herb catalogs to determine the best prices for seeds and supplies. Chart the germination and growth rate for different seeds. Survey the class and their families about scent preferences and tabulate the results. If there is a garden for the blind in your city, visit it and smell the plants. Bring soaps and shampoos from home to identify their scents. Find and create pot pourri recipes for sachets.

Step 5: Build a mini-greenhouse out of a box, wire hangers, and plastic. Plant the seeds and set up a growth chart. Tend the plants and record their development. When they are ready, harvest them and hang them in a cool, dark place to dry.

Step 6: Set up a working area to make sachets and pot pourris, and possibly scented oils too. Measure and mix homegrown and store-bought ingredients. Use natural cotton muslin bags for sachets or make your own from fabric scraps. Determine the price and create a name for your finished product. Make lightly scented oils by soaking fresh leaves of mints, rosemary, lavender, or rose petals in cold-pressed vegetable oil (try olive or peanut oil). Replace the petals or herbs every 24 hours with fresh ones for a week. Pour finished scented oils into small bottles and label them.

Step 7: Draw and write advertisements for your products and distribute ads to families and

friends or post around the school or neighborhood. Set up a table at the next science fair or crafts fair to sell them. Keep a
record of the expenses and decide what to
do with the profits.

Step 8: Write and document these entrepre-
neurial experiences. Celebrate with an
herbal feast (perhaps using some of the
recipes published in the Herbal Cookbook, mentioned in Step #1). Revise poems or personal stories of transformation
(see step #3) and form them into a collaborative book.

Fairytale Literature

This curriculum was inspired by The Cinderella Project, and Elba Marrero's work with gifted third grade students and also by writing courses taught at NYU Film School. It can be adapted to any age or level. It uses fairytales and folktales to teach literary analysis, including an introduction to comparative literature (often not introduced until the college level). It combines social studies, language arts, and art. For science Elba taught about deciduous forests (where fairies live), and for art her students made ceramic fairy realms, or milk carton fairy villages, or shoebox dioramas of fairy rooms.

> Step 1: Students are invited to bring in their favorite fairytales to share. Discuss them and the work of the Grimm Brothers and Hans Christian Andersen. Introduce fairytales from around the world and different versions of Cinderella (there are more than a dozen variations including from: Africa, Korea, the Middle East, Native America (Algonquin), China, Ireland, and the recent book and movie *Ella Enchanted*). What cultural differences are related

in the tales? Discuss movies and books that are updated or transformed versions of fairytales (such as *Edward Scissorhands* as one version of *Beauty and the Beast,* as well as the Disney musical).

Step 2: While the class discusses and compares different fairytales, make a list of all the things that you tend to find in fairytales, including plot devices and character types. What things are common to most or all of these stories (such as a wicked witch or three magic wishes)? What things are in just one or two (such as a glass slipper)? Let the children contribute as many things as they can to this list. Write it on a big pad that everyone can see.

Step 3: Congratulate the children on their brainstorming and research. Hand out an abridged list of plot changes in fairytales created by Valdimir Propp. Propp analyzed fairytales and came up with 32 plot changes they had in common. I amended this list to 16 plot changes. Students can take turns reading them aloud, and comparing them to the plot devices they put on their own list, drawn from their own analysis.

Step 4: Students take turns spontaneously creating a story by following each plot device in the Propp list. For example, the first item on the list is "A family member leaves home." One child might tell of a parent leaving for work, another might have a young man leave home to seek his fortune, another could say that the baby crawled out the door. Then it is the second student's turn. Number two is "Something is forbidden to the hero." One student chose to say, "His mommy said to not go fishing." Another might have the hero receive advice to avoid eating chocolate. Each child brings their own imagination to the table, and the storytelling gets easier and faster as the kids relax and enjoy themselves. Continue until everyone has had one or two turns and they have created an ending.

Step 5: Spontaneous storytelling occurs again, using the class-made brainstorming list along with the Propp list. The order of events is no longer important. Any child can choose any plot device or introduce any type of character, taking inspiration from either list or from his or her own imagination. Anything goes this time around. This series of storytelling warm-ups following organized research and brainstorming is a very important process to learn. It gets the students ready to write, and many will write a short fairytale or story immediately following this storytelling game. I suggest that you allow for some writing time.

Step 6: Ask the students to choose a fairytale to base theirs on, or they may use the Propp list or the list made by the group, or they may choose to rely solely on their own imaginations. They have one week to choose a fairytale as their model, or to select their main characters. They must also choose a unique setting, a definite time and place, where their story will occur. For example, one student who chose to base a story on the Ugly Duckling updated it to modern times and placed it in NYC's Central Park. Encourage students to begin writing their stories and sharing them (voluntarily) in class, even before they are finished.

Step 7: Bring in an object to inspire ideas about a fairy's world. I like to bring in acorns and acorn caps, enough for everyone. I ask the children how a fairy might use the acorn cap, and invite them to draw a picture or tell a story. My students' fairies have used acorn caps as: cups, bowls, chairs, hats, a sled, and a boat. Then I ask them to write a recipe of that fairy's favorite food, and illustrate it. If there are enough recipes we make a fairy cookbook.

Step 8: Each student can make a fairy house or they can turn the classroom into a fairy forest. Fairy houses are easily made from washed out milk cartons. Glue handmade leaf paper to the outside, and decorate with natural items: herbs, seeds, twigs, pine cone pieces, etc. Write about the fairy or fairies who live there.

Step 9: When the fairytales are completed, shared with the class, and revised, it is time to turn them into books. Each student makes a simple stick-and-elastic book using leaf paper and twigs. They print out their fairytales on computers at home and glue the pages into their homemade books. Stories can also be printed out in a miniature-sized font and made into fairy-sized books for the fairies. A collaborative book including everyone's fairytales is compiled. Titles are nominated and voted on, and illustrations are contributed. A copy is made for each student. The last day of class is presentation day, and a publishing party. Students may read aloud any selection from the book that they like, and show off their handmade books too.

Make Your Own Board Game

This is a course in writing and research aimed at grades 3-8. It was inspired by games my sons made as children, especially three increasingly difficult versions of a game on whales. All materials are inexpensive, available online at www.barebooks.com. Students love to do this work, since the ultimate goal is to make a game that anyone can play. Research skills are taught in the classroom, while outside, real-world research is encouraged as it applies to the child's interests. Students are asked to choose a subject they want to learn more about. Choices have included: the solar system, gold, Medieval European castles, cats, global warming, ancient Egypt, chocolate, dinosaurs, the Great Depression, Greek mythology, and more. In the process of following my curriculum, each child teaches his or her own to everyone else! Kids have so much fun in this course, they don't realize just how much they are learning!

> Step 1: Compare examples of popular board games, their designs and how they are played. Introduce the boards and materials (cards, dice and pawns) that the students will be using. Distribute research

materials: a large envelope with a blank lined pad and a pencil, all ready to take to the library. Children are asked to each choose a topic they are already interested in that they would like to learn more about. These possible board game topics are discussed and individual subject choices are made. The parent or teacher needs to approve the chosen topic in order to avoid too broad a choice. Then students visit a library and take out at least one book on their subject.

Step 2: Different types of resources are introduced and explained: library (books), internet search (simple and advanced), home (your own bookshelves and family), periodicals (newspapers and magazines), museums, interviews, other sites and resources (for example, a horse stable, or the telephone book). Instructions are given to make fact cards that will be necessary for their game. Students are advised to do as many kinds of research as they can, turning their notes into questions and answers.

Step 3: When at least 20 questions and answers have been written down, packs of 30 blank fact cards are handed out, with a finished sample (on another subject). In my sample I write a question in 14 pt. font (such as "What is the largest whale?"), and the answer below it upside-down in italics and 10 pt. font. I put a symbol or word on the other side of the card which will lie face up when stacked on the board (perhaps a rubber stamped image or a sticker of a whale or a quick sketch). Students have created anywhere from 30 to 100 cards, and I give them as many cards as they need. Various ways of making the cards are discussed, along with various game instructions. They do not have to copy my sample; they are encouraged to invent their own style of fact card. Students are then invited to quiz each other. In the final 15 or 20 minutes of every class, each student gets a chance to stump the rest.

Step 4: Students are instructed on how to do internet research, and shown how to do an advanced Google search. Suggestions for search phrases include their subject with the word "facts." Special site research (such as a museum or historical site) and interview-based research is discussed. The difference between primary sources, secondary sources (secondhand information), and tertiary sources is explained. Each child is given a suggested field trip or research site to support his or her chosen topic. Students continue quizzing each other, or they quiz their parents or teacher.

Step 5: Research experiences are shared. Students are instructed on how to find magazine and newspaper articles in a library archives. Specific periodicals, perhaps specific issues, are recommended or given to each student. Picture research is suggested for board decorations. A game on the Blizzard of 1888 had copies of actual newspaper photographs downloaded from the New York Times archives glued onto the game board.

Step 6: Students are given sheets of paper 18 inches square (game board size) to sketch the design of their board. On the sketches or in their lined pads, they write down what will be on each square. Some students choose a blank board on which they will draw their own path; others choose a board that already has twenty-eight squares framing the board. A square can remain blank, or show a symbol that matches the fact cards (meaning pick a card). A square can also give instructions (roll again, lose a turn, move ahead or back), or information that might help a player to answer a fact card correctly (for example, in a game about Sacajawea one square might have the date when Lewis & Clark's expedition departed).

Step 7: Board design and game rules are discussed. How does a player start? How does a player win? What happens when a player answers a fact card correctly or incorrectly? Designing the board naturally leads to ideas for the game's rules. Students decorate their fact cards and boards using rubber stamps, stickers, permanent markers, and whatever else they can think of.

Step 8: Write a draft of the board game instructions. Each set of instructions must be clear enough for anyone to understand. Instructions are tested on family members and classmates. The sketch of the board can be used for practice if the actual board isn't ready yet, and pennies or paper scraps can be temporary pawns. Feedback about game instructions is given and students are guided to make revisions.

Step 9: Complete the design and decoration of game boards. Review and revise game instructions and write the final draft. Pawns and dice are distributed along with large folders to decorate with the game's name. Students decorate wooden pawns with stickers or handmade art, or substitute pawns with other things (for example, tiny plastic horses for a game on horses, or foreign coins for a game on money).

Step 10: Play the games! This day is party day, and families are invited to attend. We set up long tables and play half or a third of the games at a time, using two or three class periods. Most students prefer to play each other's games since they know their own so well. That gives them an innate desire to make their game instructions easy to understand. Kids have so much fun in this course that they have no idea how hard they are working or how much they are learning! (*Photograph on cover is of Game Day.*)

Respecting Our Future

I have been asked what my vision would be for a model school of the future. Admittedly, I advocate homeschooling as the ideal for personal excellence. In recent years I have seen homeschool learning centers appear, often located in church basements or family homes, where children take classes part-time one or two days a week and find the rest of their learning in other places. For many families, this is the ideal. The constant stream of creative offerings and endless supply of teachers seeking to leave the school environment allows for a healthy competition. Poor teachers, often those ruined by prison-like schools, fail to attract returning students. Homeschool centers are likely to boast a fascinating array of electives far more intriguing than the standard subjects. I also recognize the growing number of democratic free schools (like Summerhill and Sudbury) and alternative schools (Reggio Emilia, Montessori, Waldorf, and more), independent schools, charter schools, special ed. schools, and the need to restructure traditional public schools. Are there any ideals that all of these different approaches and philosophies share? Is there such a thing as a model school?

When we speak of the future, it is wise to remember that it rests in the hands of the children. So I would speak to children, and ask them what makes them feel happy, spirited, and alive when they are learning. Ask them what they like least about school, and what they like most. Ask them, if they could learn anywhere, where would they go? Ask them to describe their ideal learning setting. And then ask them, if they could learn anything... what would it be?

As I suggested in the chapter Assessments, I would have each child set his or her own goals. I would ask them to do this at the beginning of the year and again during the year, perhaps prior to winter and spring breaks. Parents can also write down the goals that they have for their child. The educator's job then becomes the implementation of these goals, with the aim of helping the child achieve them, without lowering the educator's standards or compromising the child's values. It is a delicate challenge, but it is only this marriage of everyone's goals and ideals that will make everyone happy. When family, student, and teacher truly come together, each supporting each other's goals, success inevitably occurs.

A strong educational environment encourages teachers to develop their own passions, and encourages each child to develop his or hers as well. Educators can do this by individualizing many parts of the curriculum, and by inviting the children to share their enthusiasms and develop their own projects. Listen to the children and engage them. Seek to increase their active involvement whenever and however possible. Allow them the freedom of their own focus.

Include families at every opportunity. Visit their homes first and speak to them about their interests and backgrounds. Discover what they might like to contribute. Invite them in for student-led classroom interviews that naturally develop respectful relationships between students, teacher, and families. Look for unexpected opportunities and new learning experiences that each new student and family bring. Don't rely on a standardized curriculum that remains the same from year to year. Challenge yourself to make a well-used curriculum come alive in new ways that have added meaning for your students, or, better yet, trade it in for another plan, perhaps one inspired by the students themselves. If you must use out-dated texts, challenge yourself and your students to find out what is wrong with the information in these books, what is missing, or misunderstood.

A child who has a problem should never be viewed as a problem. Children often need vision therapy or physical therapy or speech therapy (as my sons did) in order to help them focus and learn. Parents should make certain that the therapists have good rapport with their child by getting referrals from families and by listening to the ever-changing needs of the child.

Tests should be used as diagnostic tools to help us guide our children to better health and success, not to grade them or label them. Make educator's assessments about personal improvement, a handwritten statement rather than a report card, words that will help inspire the child towards his or her next step. Stop subjecting our children to a humiliating, impersonal numerical ranking system!

Uncrowd the classrooms and give children the

freedom to move around. Keep the student-teacher ratio low (10:1 or better) so that instructors can remain attentive and aware of subtle changes in each child's personality, and so they can work with varied quantities: the entire classroom, small groups, and one-on-one. Maintain a safe, relaxed environment where children are comfortable enough to easily express themselves.

Seek to incorporate physical activity, humor, creative play, the visual and performing arts, and students' own original ideas into all parts of the daily curriculum. Make lesson plans, but be ready to modify them. Be ready at a moment's notice to change the lessons based on the needs and ideas of the students. Learning is best when it's an ongoing adventure that students and parent or teacher take together.

Invite the children to help in the constant re-creation of their home or school environment. Outdoors, replace the typical fenced-in playground with a science laboratory where birdhouses are built and hung, gardens are planted, and imagination and knowledge find expression. Bring classes outdoors, where math and art and writing can all occur. Indoors you would not see orderly groups of children seated at their desks, eyes ahead. Hallways would not be silent. Rather, the hum of happy activity and meaningful communication would be ever-present. Visitors peeking into classrooms might find it hard to spot the teacher. It would take them a moment of focusing on the various activities in the room to find the leader, not separate from the students, but joining in the fun.

The ultimate test of a school's success is how inclined children are to attend. When they jump out of bed in the morning and can't wait to get to school, when they do their homework without prodding, when they are excited about sharing each new idea they have and each new step in their projects, when they speak about their school and their teachers with obvious love and pride, when they clamor for school on a holiday, then you know you have a successful place of learning. The children will tell you.

Suggested Reading On Education

Albert, David H. *And the Skylark Sings With Me*, and *Homeschooling and the Voyage of Self-Discovery: A Journey of Original Seeking*. (http://www.skylarksings.com/)

Armstrong, Dr. Thomas. *Multiple Intelligences, Awakening Your Child's Natural Genius*, and *You're Smarter Than You Think*. (http://thomasarmstrong.com/)

Bauer, Susan Wise, & Jessie Wise. *The Well-Trained Mind: A Guide to Classical Education at Home*.

Brown, Resa Steindel. *A Call to Brilliance*

Colfax, David & Micki. *Hard Times in Paradise*.

Dancy, Rahima Baldwin. *You Are Your Child's First Teacher*.

Freire, Paulo. *Pedagogy of the Oppressed*.

Gatto, John Taylor. *Dumbing Down Our Schools*, and *The Underground History of American Education*. (http://johntaylorgatto.com/)

Goleman, Daniel. *Emotional Intelligence: Why it can matter more than IQ*.

Holt, John. *Teach Your Own*, and *Learning All the Time*. (http://www.holtgws.com/index.html)

Kealuha, Anna. *Trust the Children*.

Kindle-Hodson, & Victoria, & Mariaemma Willis. *Discover Your Child's Learning Style.*

Koch, Kenneth. *Wishes, Lies and Dreams.*

Kohl, Herbert R. *The Open Classroom*, and *36 Children.*

Lamb, Albert, & A. S. Neill. *Summerhill School: A New View of Childhood.*

Langer, Ellen. *The Power of Mindful Learning.*

Leistico, Agnes. *I Learn Better by Teaching Myself.*

Levine, Mel. *A Mind at a Time*, and *The Myth of Laziness.*

Llewellyn, Grace, & Amy Silver. *Guerrilla Learning: How to Give Your Kids a Real Education With or Without School.*

Llewellyn, Grace. *The Teenage Liberation Handbook.*

McKee, Alison. *Homeschooling Our Children, Unschooling Ourselves.*

Montessori, Maria. *The Absorbent Mind.*

Neill, A. S. *Summerhill: A Radical Approach to Child Rearing.*

Pearce, Joseph Chilton. *The Magical Child.*

Ratey, John J. *Spark: The Revolutionary New Science of Exercise and the Brain.*

Rivero, Lisa. *Creative Home Schooling for Smart Families.*

Rogovin, Paula. *Classroom Interviews: A World of Learning*.

Rodari, Gianni. *The Grammar of Fantasy*.

Sheffer, Susannah. *A Sense of Self: Listening to Home-schooled Adolescent Girls*.

Sklar, Daniel Judah. *Playmaking: Children Writing and Performing Their Own Plays*.

Sliverman, Linda Kreger. *Upside-Down Brilliance: The Visual-Spatial Learner*.

Smith, Frank. *The Book of Learning & Forgetting*.

Warner, Sylvia Ashton. *Teacher*.

Zull, James. *The Art of Changing the Brain: Enriching the Practice of Teaching by Exploring the Biology of Learning*.

Visit http://HomeschoolNYC.com/

Where you will find:

Articles by the author,
Information on homeschooling,
Hundreds of free educational activities in New York City,
Travel ideas and unusual summercamps in the NYC area,
Recommended books and resources on every subject,
Thousands of interesting links.

About the Author

Born in Madison, Wisconsin to university professors, Laurie Block Spigel grew up in New York City, where she and her husband homeschooled their two children. Her sons were later accepted to their first choice colleges with generous scholarships. Today Laurie teaches groups of homeschoolers, specializing in playwriting, poetry, literature and art history. She also lectures and leads workshops for parents and teachers on child-led learning and innovative education, and works as an educational consultant. Through her website, www.HomeschoolNYC.com, she continues to help and inform NYC parents. Laurie lives in NYC with her husband, Jerry, who operates a gallery of Native American Art. In her spare time Laurie enjoys books, photography, and travel. She is currently working on a book for children.